LOVE IN
THE DARK

LOVE IN THE DARK

PHILOSOPHY BY ANOTHER NAME

DIANE ENNS

Columbia University Press   *New York*

Columbia University Press
Publishers Since 1893
New York   Chichester, West Sussex
cup.columbia.edu
Copyright © 2016 Columbia University Press
All rights reserved

Library of Congress Cataloging-in-Publication Data
Names: Enns, Diane, author.
Title: Love in the dark : philosophy by another name / Diane Enns.
Description: New York : Columbia University Press, 2016. |
Includes bibliographical references and index.
Identifiers: LCCN 2016003652 (print) | LCCN 2016015401 (ebook) |
ISBN 9780231178969 (cloth : alk. paper) | ISBN 9780231542098
(e-book) | ISBN 9780231542098 ()
Subjects: LCSH: Love.
Classification: LCC BD436 .E65 2016 (print) | LCC BD436 (ebook) |
DDC 128/.46—dc23
LC record available at https://lccn.loc.gov/2016003652

Columbia University Press books are printed on permanent and
durable acid-free paper.
This book is printed on paper with recycled content.
Printed in the United States of America

c 10 9 8 7 6 5 4 3 2 1

Cover image: © Daniel Fast

References to websites (URLs) were accurate at the time of writing.
Neither the author nor Columbia University Press is responsible
for URLs that may have expired or changed since
the manuscript was prepared.

For my friends

CONTENTS

Contents ✤ ix

PREFACE

WHEN we love, we move in the dark. One love is unlike another. We make our way without landmarks to guide us, our old loves shedding little light on new loves. In this sense, love is blind indeed.

This might explain our pleasure in telling stories of love over and over again, believing that repetition will settle love into templates and give rise to formulas. But there are no formulas for love. Every event of love becomes its own story, told in as many ways as human forms of expression allow.

When we try to understand love, we do so from under the skin of our own experience. What happens to us in love—or fails to happen—appears in the lines we write or between them. The novelist disguises her stories in the lives of imagined characters, beneath the thin veil separating art from autobiography. The poet may bury his secrets in metaphor or run naked across the page, risking all.

And the philosopher? We have our stories, too.

"When you are in the middle of a story it isn't a story at all, but only a confusion," writes Margaret Atwood, "a dark roaring, a blindness, a wreckage of shattered glass and splintered wood."

Only later when you are telling it does it become anything like a story.[1] In the telling, we impose order on disorder through the conventions of language and draw generalities from particulars with the assurances that knowledge provides. We remember; we tell the story as though everything happened transparently, with purpose. We find convenient patterns. Yet something of life always slips through the cracks of this ordering, like the poem that escapes the confines of linguistic conventions. Something of the "dark roaring" of an event resists all attempts at synthesis; we feel it rumble, hear it echo. Erotic love is especially rebellious in this respect; human vulnerability and the intensity of our intimate attachments do not permit assurances.

How can the philosopher write of love in the face of this roaring and rebellion, when the tools of the trade are logic and rational argument and the desire is for certainty? She tries to settle love into neat theories and fails, for love cannot be abstracted from flesh, blood, and sensation, from the surge of emotion we experience in the presence of the beloved—a surge that propels us beyond ourselves to experience as far as possible life lived in another's body. We can write of love only in the first person, if not explicitly, then obliquely. We write as if we are others to ourselves, two skinless interlocutors in conversation, swept along in a steady flow of words.

Overburdened by the Western tradition and its celebrated and protected masculine lineage—by what I call *philosophy proper*—the professional philosopher is confounded by erotic love. Plato began the story by extricating love from the human body and emotion. Ever since then, philosophers have tended to cower in the face of intense emotions—small demons over which we have little control—taking refuge in a Reason purged of feeling. Like surgeons with their scalpels, they prefer to work in a sterilized environment, intent on precision but often indifferent to the life of the particular body before them. Love, in all its maddening vicissitudes, is left to the musing of poets and musicians, whose melodies act like watery conduits for the emotions love elicits, making us laugh or weep in sympathy.

Indecent exposure is required. In the revelation, we meet others, for our emotions are never original even if the event that gave rise to them is singular. And so we find our own experiences of grief or joy mirrored on the pages that describe another's. Who is entitled to write in the first person, Alexander Herzen asks in *My Past and Thoughts*, to write memoir or autobiography—"reminiscences," as he calls them? "Everyone," he replies, "because no one is obliged to read them." It is not necessary to be great, notorious, or celebrated, he explains; it is enough to be human, to have a story to tell and some ability to tell it, for "every life is interesting." We write in the first person because "man likes to enter into another existence, he likes to touch the subtlest fibres of another's heart, and to listen to its beating . . . he compares, he checks it by his own, he seeks for himself confirmation, sympathy, justification."[2]

We seek such confirmation to break the isolation of our own inner life, our emotions, our incessant internal dialogue, our heartaches. We rest our head on another's chest and feel our existence affirmed in the heartbeat we find there. We look deep into another's eyes to confirm the depth of our own.

My philosopher friend says to me, "When I read you, I feel as though I can touch you." Yes, this is why I write, I tell him, to touch and to be touched, to meet another momentarily on a page, my words an invitation into the undercurrents of a life. This is the erotic opening of writing and thinking. I want to read a philosopher I can touch, whose life is fully present in the work and draws me in. A work with a pulse that quickens my own.

A work unconstrained by arbitrary divisions between experience and ideas, emotion and reason, poetry and philosophy. A naked work, having shed the layers of clothing with which we protect ourselves from the elements, the barriers between ideas and the life that gives birth to them. I want the beauty of reflection that proper philosophy too often forgoes in favor of a certain logic. I want resonance and understanding rather than argument, to be moved rather than to be certain.

Following Hélène Cixous, I wish to reverse the mandate of philosophy—to find truth in the concept—by returning relevance and priority to those passions that begin in the "innumerable turbulences of the soul." We begin with *material*, she writes, with something that happens, and before everything becomes "crystallized" in a word or a narrative, we "paint" phenomena with poetic writing. While theory is indispensable, it is a dangerous "prosthesis"—"what is most true is naked life."[3]

We might call this "philosophy by another name," signaling a departure from the tradition and practice of philosophy proper, its monological face turned away from eros. The activity of thinking demands creativity and movement, to live in the passionate moment of the "why," always present to the world. I look to those thinkers who remain faithful to the restlessness of eros, their appetite for the work of thinking and understanding an unstoppable force in life.

No one captures this force better than Anne Carson in an analogy based on Franz Kafka's short story about a philosopher who spends his spare time around children so he can grab the spinning tops with which they play. He wants to understand the spinning of the top, the "impertinent" way it defies normality, but as soon as he catches it, he feels sick. Carson suggests that to catch beauty is not the point; it is the yearning after it, the running after the spinning top, that gives us pleasure. "Beauty spins and the mind moves," she explains. "To catch beauty would be to understand how that impertinent stability in vertigo is possible. But no, delight need not reach so far. To be running breathlessly, but not yet arrived, is itself delightful, a suspended moment of living hope." The philosopher does not run after tops in order to understand; he has become a philosopher to have an excuse for running after spinning tops. He pursues the sheer delight of pursuit.[4]

In Carson's reading of Kafka's story, eros expands, understood in a broader sense than sexual love. This is eros as a force or magnetic pull that draws us outside of ourselves to converge not only with other individuals—with varying degrees of intimacy—but also with ideas and with the worlds we create and inhabit. We rise above the boundaries of our selves, our bodies, our circumstances and immediately collide with other beings and things. Eros is the force that keeps us pursuing what is external to us mentally and physically. We crave the touch and warmth of another's body not simply for orgasmic pleasure but for the sheer pleasure of proximity and touch, no different from the infant who cries when bereft of the arms that enfold her, when surrounded only by the unbearable freedom of air. Our minds are similarly enfolded by the thinking of others and seduced by the compulsion to understand. We do not create ideas on our own but in conversation with the books we read and with the minds we encounter. Eros is what keeps us searching.

When we understand eros in this way, we will recognize its presence in much more than what we call romantic love, wherever we find ourselves reluctant to part from what is beloved. For example, we find eros in the company of well-loved friends whom we are loath to leave at the end of an afternoon. Affectionate gestures are the manifestation of a certain erotic desire, not for sexual satisfaction but for the simple pleasure of mutual affinity and *lovability*. Eros appears in the way our friends invite us into their confidences, the worlds of their emotions and sufferings, and in the beauty of their beloved faces. We can feel similarly about the erotic pull into a book or a painting or a forest, so absorbed by our sensual response that everything else recedes. We do ourselves a great disservice in reducing the pleasure of erotic intimacy to that which involves our genitalia. The astounding range of our senses and emotions defies the categories into which we seek to subdue them.

Philosophy by another name, then: reflection on the material of life. Love is not beyond thinking. But it requires the kind of thinking that bends, that accepts the limits of reason and takes the risk of moving beyond the order of the reasonable to the confusion of the emotional; here we find a rich terrain for philosophical reflection. These pages are my answer to Tim Lilburn's question "How to be here?"—How to be here in such a way that we do not "strangle the convulsive erotic energy of philosophy"?[5]

We might also ask, How to *love* without strangling the convulsive energy of eros?

I populate the following pages with the thinkers and writers in whose work I have found an answer to this question. With their help, I have learned to wade through my own light and dark in matters of love. They refuse to sacrifice the dangers of eros for the liberal scripts of "happy love," to quote Gillian Rose. "Keep your mind in hell and despair not," she reminds her readers throughout her provocative memoir, *Love's Work: A Reckoning with Life*, paying homage to the force that more than any other can bring us to the heights of ecstasy and the depths of despair, sometimes within the same day or even hour.[6] Against the liberal dream of perfect unions, against the legacies of the Western Christian and philosophical traditions with their fear of the body (woman's in particular), I want to meditate on the experience of love *in the dark*—mine specifically, but not only mine. Love that is blind thanks to its absolute singularity and irreplaceability. Love that defies any normalizing, explanatory grid we impose on it.

There is a story of love here or, rather, several, but my intent, more than a description of a past event for its own sake, is to draw insights from what has passed and invite conversations on the ideas that emerge. Thinking that begins from human experience clings to the barest facts of existence, but it does not end there. There is a kind of writing whose purpose is to describe beauty— when words perform like paintings or landscapes. And there is writing that moves us, tapping into deep emotional reserves, working the words like orchestras work the notes of a piece of music. Then there is writing that invites conversation because it pushes us beyond description to the unsettling realm of the question, where we are forced to grapple with our assumptions and prejudices. Not very often, a written work accomplishes all of these things.

I write to understand and to invite others into the work of understanding. This is always a creative process, whether we seek to understand a written text or an experience before anything has been said about it. We build worlds through conversation, just as we build a world through love. F. O. Matthiessen wrote to his lover, Russell Cheney, in the 1920s: "Of course this life of ours is entirely new—neither of us knows a parallel case. We stand in the middle of an uncharted, uninhabited country. That there have been other unions like ours is obvious, but we are unable to draw on their experience. We must create everything for ourselves. And creation is never easy."[7] This applies not only to gay lovers living their love in secret but also to all who love. We build something out of nothing when we love, and what we build is unique, unpredictable, and changeable, its end unknowable. Love, like thinking, is a creative force—we must learn how to be artists of our singular attachments.

This is also a work of mourning; a work that betrays the longing to immortalize a momentous love, just as we long to immortalize an idea, a person, a moment of insight or inspiration in the words we set down on a page. Are not all works of literature or philosophy memorials in this sense? In David Grossman's wrenching account of grief, *Falling Out of Time*, his characters speak of the necessity of writing in the process of mourning, their words immortalizing what they cannot bear to lose definitively. "Centaur," who mourns the death of his child, laments, "I cannot understand this thing that happened, nor can I fathom the person I am now, after it happened. And what's worse . . . if I do not write it, I cannot understand who *he* is now either—my son." What good would it do to write, he muses? What else is there to say but the facts, that at

> such and such time comma in
> this and that place comma my son
> comma my only child comma aged
> eleven and a half
> period the boy
> is gone
> period[8]

Gone but immortalized in the words Centaur feels compelled to speak.

When a story ends badly, Cixous writes in her notebook, we must tell it differently.[9] We must turn tragedy into something beautiful.

ACKNOWLEDGMENTS

E VERY thought in this book was discussed with my dearest friends, every story told, and every event analyzed. I dedicate this book to them.

I am grateful beyond words to Brian Phillips for inspiring conversations on the ideas in this book, enlivened by his wit, intellectual passion, and magnanimous spirit; to Fadi Abou-Rihan for opening windows with his insights when doors closed, for his gift of seeing things otherwise; and to Antonio Calcagno for hospitality that exceeds any definition we might give that term. Brian and Antonio read this work in its draft stages and commented with their usual acuity; I feel deeply indebted to them.

I wish to express my appreciation for the students, friends, and family members who analyzed with me the complexities of love relationships—whether mine or theirs—over the past few years, especially Emily Brown, Shannon Buckley, Amalie Enns, Karen Enns, Alexia Hannis, Graham Knight, Wendy McKeen, Felix Ó Murchadha, and Tristan Sibley. Some of the students who passed through my course on the philosophy of love make anonymous appearances in the pages that follow; I am grateful for their contributions. All of these individuals helped me clarify my ideas and remember that the experience of love is always resistant to clarification.

A special thanks goes to Laura Benacquista for her assistance with the final manuscript preparation and to Rabia Awan and Kim Squissato for kindness and support well beyond what their jobs require of them. I am deeply grateful to Wendy Lochner, Christine Dunbar, and the rest of the team at Columbia University Press, without whom this work would still be a notebook, and for the thoughtful comments of two anonymous reviewers.

Some material from parts 1, 2, and 3 were previously published in "Love's Limit," chapter 2 of *Thinking About Love: Essays in Contemporary Continental Philosophy*, ed. Diane Enns and Antonio Calcagno (University Park: Penn State University Press, 2015). An earlier version of "Survival," in part III of this book, originally appeared in "Love, Life, Death, and Survival," *Mosaic: A Journal for the Interdisciplinary Study of Literature* 48, no. 3 (2015): 47–55. I wish to thank Penn State University Press and *Mosaic*'s editor, Dawne McCance, for permission to reuse this content.

Finally, I would like to thank my son, Daniel Fast, for providing the perfect word here and there. And for conversations that provoke and inspire in all the right ways.

LOVE IN
THE DARK

PART I

LEGACY

RUINED STATES

WRITING begins with loss, Hélène Cixous tells us. When you are lost, beside yourself, defenseless, "without skin, inundated with otherness," this is when writings surge forth. We are like ruined states, she says, "without armies, without mastery, without ramparts." And in this condition of unmitigated exposure, we write, breathlessly, risking all, like lovers.[1]

I start at the end. Which is really a beginning, as all endings are. When we are in the middle of the ending, we do not know that a beginning lies in wait, impatient to be born. But we do not want to know. Anything but that, we plead into the darkness of our interregnum.

Then there is the epiphany, a sudden revelation or a slow drumming from beneath our skins, where that fetal beginning makes her presence known.

It was that Tuesday morning. Your face—indifferent mask of turmoil—turned away from me as I said good-bye and kissed your unyielding cheek. But I knew, despite my stubborn denial, that you had reached the outer limit, the point of no return, because you were deaf to me and exultant in your deafness. There was only one story that would absolve you, and it was not mine. You longed only for the sweet relief of my departure, a blood-letting as calming as it was violent. There is a moment when the torment of love seems worse than the torment of abandon-ment. I heard in your actions Abelard's parting words to Héloise: "How happy shall I be if I thus lose you!"[2] In the vain fullness of my denial, I said, "See you next week."

So I left and did not return.

I would never have believed that love might not be enough until it wasn't.

WHAT IS LOVE?

"What is love?" has never been my question. I have never won-dered whether I love. It was always a given, as any affective state of being, without need of definition. I did not have to ask, as many do, How do I know when I am in love?

Love is an emotion, probably our most powerful, although hate might be equal to it. This hardly simplifies things, for our affective lives are far more complex than our reasoning lives. We found attitudes on the power of our emotions, attitudes that ori-ent us toward or away from the world. Resentment, rage, hate, love affect how we experience every event that surprises us and every relation in which we find ourselves. It is not reductive, then, to define love as an emotion, for an emotion is no small thing. The fact that we so often grant to love a godly status, as though it transcends "mere" human feeling, affirms rather than denies the power of our emotions.

Although everyone has an emotive life (with maybe a few exceptions), we feel our emotions with varying degrees of intensity and awareness. Some of us are more attuned to our emotions at any given moment, feel some or all of them more powerfully than do others, and hold them in higher esteem. I am one such person, long practiced in contemplating my own and others' emotive states. Maybe this is why I never had to ask what love is, for I always knew when and whom I loved, starting with Mr. Dressup—master of children's imaginative television—and the boy I kissed behind the door in kindergarten.

Most of the time when we ask what love is and whether we love, the real questions are, Do I want a relationship with this person, and what kind of relationship? This is not to ask what I feel for someone, but whether my feelings match those sanctioned by this or that type of relationship. Then we wonder if this feeling is friendship love or sexual love, whether we want a long-term relationship or a brief one, a fling or a family. Discussions of romantic love are generally discussions of relationships rather than of love itself. For example, to say that love is love only if it lasts forever is merely a statement about our respect for longevity in relationships. Love, like hate, *might* last forever, but there are many experiences of love—maybe most—that do not. Similarly, we say that love is hard work, when in fact it is relationships and cohabiting that are hard work. To parent with someone requires an altogether different skill set than what love might generate. In this sense, we inflate the term *love*, recognizing the sheer magnitude of its scope. With excessive inflation, love becomes a spiritual entity or ideal, and it comes to bear little relation to what we feel when we love.

When thinking about what love is, *in itself*—what constitutes this emotion and what its effects are—we work against powerful legacies. If the force of human love is displaced in the Christian tradition by God's inexhaustible love, leaving an empty self who yearns to be loved and lovable, in the liberal tradition love's force is sterilized and institutionalized, its fundamental condition an autonomous self worthy of love from another autonomous self. The liberal ideal of love is not transcendent in the Christian sense—projecting a perfect love onto a perfect Being—but similarly split between a perfect love and its defective imitation. Liberal love is dependent on symmetry in equality and autonomy between two persons. Measured by endurance and longevity, it is not supposed to fail. In this way, our ideals of love have been shaped by the Western Christian tradition, and we fool ourselves if we think in our secular age we have moved beyond it.

Liberal love is a seductive ideal, easy to market; we find it in all our best contemporary descriptions of ideal couple love. Irving Singer offers a particularly appealing vision of romantic love, characterized by mutual respect, care, and the desire to please. The value bestowed freely on another when we love causes both lover and beloved to be created anew into augmented versions of their original selves. There is receptivity and responsiveness, reciprocal delight and sustenance.[3] In Alain de Botton's ideal version, the couple's love must be "mature." This pristine form of love is marked by an active awareness of the good and the bad in each person; it is full of temperance, resists a superficial idealization of the beloved, is free of jealousy, masochism, or obsession. Mature love is pleasant, peaceful, and reciprocated. De Botton describes this love briefly at the end of a poignant story of a relationship characterized by idealization and dependency that ends with infidelity. Mature love is like the antidote for diseased love—discovered after loving the "wrong" person and failing to achieve happiness. Not surprisingly, given our cultural dictates, but surprisingly given de Botton's demystification of love throughout the story, he surmises that mature love logically ends in marriage.[4]

Liberal accounts of romantic love idealize the context or conditions thought necessary for love to occur. The ideal lovers are equal in their capacity for love, for generosity, and for intimacy. The essential condition for this reciprocal love is a strong, autonomous, or sovereign self, vulnerable enough to let the other in, yet secure enough in itself to be free of jealousy—a self sufficiently able to recognize a lover's needs but equally able to demand generosity. This self knows itself as a discrete entity and is therefore thought capable of valuing and being valued by another such discrete self.

There is nothing intrinsically wrong with these ideals. Singer's notion of love as bestowing value on another is quite beautiful, unusually focused on what the lover gains in loving rather than in being loved. Singer alludes to the larger world engendered by the valuation that occurs through love: "In responding affirmatively to another person, the lover creates something and need lose nothing in himself. To bestow value is to augment one's own being as well as the beloved's. Bestowal generates a new society by the sheer force of emotional attachment, a society that enables the lovers to discard many of the conventions that would ordinarily have separated them."[5] This is a moving depiction of a mutually affirming world created between two lovers.

But I am skeptical of the ideal conditions that such visions of love presuppose. The logical conclusion is that we do not experience love when our love is not reciprocated. We do not love when we love jealously, obsessively, or when we shamelessly abandon ourselves to another. It is not authentic love when we love those who have wronged us, who are psychologically wounded and love us within limits. These *actual* experiences of love—that is, love mixed with other emotions, love between imperfect individuals in uncertain circumstances—are pathologized within a liberal worldview. We have learned to dismiss love as the product of our blind imaginations or to reduce love to a pathology arising from the mysterious recesses of the unconscious. This reduction is particularly acute when the object of one's love is deemed unworthy—by the relationship "experts," the psychotherapy industry, or even well-meaning friends—as though love is love only when the beloved is wholly lovable, when lover and beloved are equal in their capacity to love, and, above all, when they subscribe to a liberal version of autonomy. If love is not an equal exchange between two such deserving, sovereign selves, we tend to call it something else: masochism, repetition compulsion, fantasy, or an unhealthy attachment. This reduction may acknowledge the force of love, but it gives the unconscious too much determining power, reducing the emotions associated with love to mere symptoms of sinister, secret desires. And so we learn, again and again, to mistrust our feelings for another as we search for what we think we *should* desire.

If love itself is an emotion—intense, unruly, waxing and waning, and sometimes dissipating altogether for good reason or none at all—the terms of our understanding shift. There is no ideal against which we must measure our emotions, no "true love" outside of the truth of our emotional response to another person. All love is true, then, no matter how intensely felt, because anything that we feel is not false—emotions are not measurable in terms of truth or falsity. All love is true, but not all love is propelled by the same force, the same emotional intensity. Love is only as complex as the person who feels it and the person to whom it is directed. Like other emotions, love may take on a life of its own that becomes bigger than the one who feels it. This is not a transcendent love in the Christian sense, for there is nothing to repudiate—body, lust, pleasure; love rises from one body to embrace another. The emotion can overwhelm us, affect us beyond the immediate world of the relation of two. In this, Singer is absolutely right: love provides us with meaning. Love enhances, augments, affirms. When we lose love, it is the memory of this augmented life that overcomes us in our grieving. We recall the pleasure or pain of the emotions that permeated our lives with a loved one; we recall that movement outside of ourselves, that irresistible pull into another's inner life.

Everyone's experience of love has a complicated individual genealogy that winds through conscious and unconscious events and encounters with the complicated genealogies of others' love lives. As if this were not difficult enough, these entangled genealogies also arise out of a greater collective history of the conditions for love.

ANARCHIC EROS

Erotic love began for me in the abyss between the sanctioned and the illicit. I was hounded on one side by the stern representatives of a Christian God and on the other by eros. In between reigned a confusion of guilt and pleasure. The ministers were armed with a congregation's unshakeable belief in their direct line to God, inflated by the certainty of their own virtue. They laid down the law with the phallic power granted to them, as though they were one with it. But eros had no law, no phallic lineage to recommend it. Eros flowed in our veins—hot, anarchic.

The ministers read Paul's letters to the early Christians from a red pulpit while we sat on spiteful benches in our summer dresses, inviting admiration from the suited young men lining the balcony opposite us. We daydreamed to the backdrop of a voice relaying Paul's exhortations against the sins of the flesh. Everywhere was this word *flesh*, with its equal measure of prohibition and incitement:[6]

If you are not "men of God," you are "men of the flesh" (I Cor. 3:1–4).[7]

Is there jealousy and strife? Then you are still "of the flesh" (I Cor. 3:1–4).

"Flesh and blood cannot inherit the kingdom of God" (I Cor. 15:50).

"'The spirit is indeed willing but the flesh is weak'" (Matt. 26:41).

It is well for a man not to touch a woman, we were warned, and for the unmarried and the widowed to remain single like Paul (I Cor. 7:1, 8). But rather than submit to the temptations of the flesh, it would be better to marry. From the restless church balconies came sighs of relief, for Paul advised that marriage is preferable to a life "aflame with passion" (I Cor. 7:9). Each man should have his own wife and each woman her own husband to resist the temptation to immorality (I Cor. 7:2). We must have ignored the contradiction: in our naive hearts, we thought that choosing marriage *was* choosing a life of passion. But questions and contradictions were prohibited in our black-and-white world. And so institution won over passion, as it so often does.

We forgot Paul's exhortations anyway in moments of hot breath and searching hands. In the dark, we lusted or loved; illicit exploration after dusk in parked cars or, once, in the church sanctuary after the faithful had gone home, under the watchful eyes of God. Holy indulgence—this was the contradiction of the abyss that left us ecstatic and confused at the same time. The flesh has its own will, we discovered—it was anything but weak—and the body has its own truth: irrepressible eros.

Did we feel guilt or only pretend to feel it, obliged by the law of Paul? How could the exhilaration of touch give way to guilt? If thy right hand offends thee, Matthew wrote, then cut it off (Matt. 5:30). The boys might have thought of this when they reached for our breasts, but eros proved to be more powerful than ancient admonitions, and guilt served as sufficient punishment until the next time. We were being what we were—skin and hair, mouth and hand, eye and mind. Giving and receiving. For at sixteen I was in love with a boy, our minds as aflame as our bodies. He suffered as only Augustine could suffer, violently torn between his aspiration for transcendence and his desire for the girl who shared his passions. So the ministers counseled him: avoid sin by not wrapping the sheets too tightly at night.

And the girl? I was already condemned by Eve's decision, sentenced with all female bodies to exile on the wrong side of the law. More familiar with our own blood, we were closer to that flesh Paul spurned. Always-already barred from the realm of transcendence and its perks. But our secret was to know that eros could be sacred—our bodies were temples, the ministers told us. Paul said, "Do you not know that your body is a temple of the Holy Spirit within you, which you have from God? You are not your own; you were bought with a price. So glorify God in your body" (I Cor. 6:19–20). We were pleased to carry within us this holiness. Like the Catholic girl in Flannery O'Connor's "A Temple of the Holy Ghost," we felt as if someone had given us a gift.[8] It did not occur to us that this gift was rather a theft. We were *bought with a price*; to be a temple of the Holy Spirit, we had to give up our content, our soul. We had to give up eros, pure gift without any price, sacred eros coming to us from elsewhere, taking possession, contracting our muscles, and moistening our skin.

The conflict between head and heart, will and passion, spirit and flesh was as familiar as the daily habit of praying to an imaginary being we believed loved us more than our parents. But in my youthful love for a passionate boy, in both its sanctioned and its illicit elements, were all the gifts that love brings to us: pleasure, beauty, stimulation, passion, the warmth of another body, communion with another mind, and the inevitable encounter with another's unconscious. We built a world around us, naive, exclusive, complicated, but beautiful.

We felt this at the time, I suppose, although it did not help when we were caught kissing in the garage by an aunt visiting from the old country—a "disapprover" if there ever was one, to borrow from Miriam Toews.[9]

God, Jesus, Mary, and the disciples evidently never experienced erotic passion, so they could hardly help us understand its rush and confusion. We lived our double lives, grateful for their forgiveness.

THE CANNIBAL HUSBANDS
OF OUR FUTURES

If the women felt any dissatisfaction with their lot in the Bible, they were reminded that Paul instructed husbands to love their wives. The mere suggestion put Paul leaps and bounds ahead of the men of the Old Testament. Consider Lot, who offered his virgin daughters to the thugs at the door so they would not harm his male visitors. "Do to them as you please," Lot said, "only do nothing to these men, for they have come under the shelter of my roof" (Gen. 19:8).[10] The law of hospitality evidently did not extend to one's daughters.

Paul admonished men to love their wives even while they ruled over them. As Christ is the head of the church, the husband is the head of his wife, so she must be subject "in everything" to her husband. But Paul also stipulated that husbands must love their wives "as Christ loved the church and gave himself up for her, that he might sanctify her, having cleansed her by the washing of water with the word, that he might present the church to himself in splendor, without spot or wrinkle or any such thing, that she might be holy and without blemish" (Eph. 5:24–27). A husband's love thus sanctifies his wife; she is washed clean of flaws only thanks to his love. The credit belongs to him. And here is the heart of the matter as it was presented to us at countless weddings: husbands should love their wives as they love their own bodies, for "he who loves his wife loves himself. . . . 'For this reason a man shall leave his father and mother and be joined to his wife, and the two shall become one flesh.' This mystery is a profound one, and I am saying that it refers to Christ and the church; however let each one of you love his wife as himself, and let the wife see that she respects her husband" (Eph. 5:28, 31–33).

The mystery held us in thrall until the full import of being one flesh hit us, later, much later. As the slave should be grateful for a benevolent master who rules without beating, a woman should be grateful for the love of a husband who rules over her with a God-like compassion. She is nurtured and cherished but also commanded to obey. This is the love of a Christian God and husband. Disobey and love will be withdrawn. The husband is told to love his wife. She is told to respect her husband. But the love a ruler has for his subjects is without respect. And to respect one's master is not to love him. Love without respect might rather be benevolence or kindness. Even a tyrant can be kind when he so chooses. A slave owner is kind to his slaves not because he sees in them human beings worthy of respect but because if he shows kindness, it reflects well on him. He feels better for it. The master cares for his subjects in order to serve himself, for they will work harder to please him. This benevolence does not change the fact that he controls their day-to-day lives and determines their fates. To respect his subjects would entail giving up this control over life itself. Conversely, respect for a master without love is not respect but obedience, which negates love. For when we obey, we do not love freely, but under duress, which is not love but fearful regard.

In Paul's version of conjugal love, husband and wife do not become one flesh but one self, and it is the husband's self that the two become. This relation does not sustain her; it sustains him. He feeds on his wife's devotion; as her self diminishes, his engorges. A figurative cannibalism.

Hannah Arendt once said, "Strictly speaking, he who does not love and desire at all is a nobody."[11] But we girls were taught that to love we must suppress desire and *become* nobodies. Woman has no body in this picture except that which operates as exchange value—no self she can call her own. For a woman to love is to declare, "I am no body." For a man to love is to declare, "I am the world—the world exists through me and I am no longer one 'this' among other 'thises.'"[12] And woman complies, making him the world.

For such a long time I conflated respect with fear.

TWO CRUCIFIXIONS

Susan Sontag wrote in her notebooks, "What I have to get over: the idea that the value of love rises as the self dwindles."[13]

In Christian love, the self is emptied into another. This love is a nonreciprocal gift that cancels out the giver. In the person of Jesus, persecuted, mutilated, and executed, we find our enduring symbol of self-sacrifice, perhaps the product of our unconscious fantasies of unconditional mother love and disappointment with its actuality. This is love without limits, love as God's inexhaustible grace and mercy, love as the very definition of God. It is no longer we who love—bodies and minds intertwining, passions fusing—but God who loves through us. We are merely empty vessels, striving to be worthy of God's love. In this way, Christianity erodes all agency in human love and denies the passions from which it arises—the passions that propel us beyond ourselves. How comforting to be fortified against the storm of human love, against the fear of its power, its ambivalence, against grief over its loss. We are foiled by God; human love appears weak and passive, uncertain and conditional. If our emotions and passions must be denied, our love is insignificant. But without them, there is no self who loves.

Once a month at communion we drank the blood of Jesus in tiny glasses filled with red grape juice (wine was sinful—like dancing, it could lead to other things) and ate his flesh in the form of unleavened bread. Metaphoric cannibalism again. The flesh of his body was inescapable —a body nailed to a cross, blood dripping from open hands torn by nails and from a forehead pierced by a crown of thorns —but it was a body destroyed, an act of annihilation repeated by generations of theologians and philosophers. The only violence and cruelty I was exposed to as a girl, given our restricted television hours, were those images of Jesus dying on the cross. Bleeding but forgiving, suffering in silence, but with eyes that expressed all the agony of the human condition. Be filled with awe, we were instructed, that the son of God could love us with such mercy despite our wickedness. How powerful were those images—forever fixed on the walls of our minds. Cruelty and death, blood, gore, suffering, sacrifice, martyrdom—these were the images that accompanied the Christian love story.

Impressionable youth, we soaked it up. Emptying ourselves that we might be filled. Love was suffering in response to cruelty. Jesus did not rebel; he obeyed his omnipotent Father, who orchestrated his death for the good of others. The Mary presented to us suffered without protest; she played a minor role in our faith—she was a Mennonite Mary, not a Catholic Mary, a surrogate mother for God's child, sacrificed to tragedy. Depicted as beatific or downcast, saintly, weepy. To us, she was lifeless, an image without content. Yet we all wanted to play the part of Mennonite Mary in the Nativity play at Christmas, trying to look suitably holy as we stood quietly next to Joseph, a wrapped doll in a makeshift manger between us. This was the life we imagined in the Family Trinity: our desires reached no further than to be Mary—mute, docile, adoring, a model of passivity. Empty and waiting to be filled by husband and infant.

We girls were masochists in the making, nothing without God. We absorbed this teaching through every sentient pore of our bodies. In the vast stillness of the church, we begged God to use us, empty and worthless as we were, inhaling his unconditional love, exhaling our nothingness. So we cried over Christ's bleeding hands and forehead, emulating his long-suffering mother.

For who else could we emulate? There were the prostitutes who washed Jesus's feet with their tears and hair, the raped daughters of the Old Testament, ugly, unloved Leah and her beautiful but barren sister Rachel. These were our choices. The boys could look to the disciples of Jesus as their role models, mimic their camaraderie as they ate and talked together, share their divine purpose in disseminating truth to the masses and providing a line to God for those less fortunate. But the only woman in Jesus's inner circle was Mary Magdalene, a prostitute, or so we were told; he had no girlfriends for us to aspire to, or at least we never heard about them. Neither did the disciples, and Paul was very clear his bed would not be shared. There was Eve, of course, but enough has been said about her—evil temptress, the woman held solely responsible for the destruction of the idyllic garden we might otherwise inhabit.

Only gutless Mary was ours to claim. We were given no explanation for how a virgin could become pregnant, but I don't remember wondering about it. For all we knew, God was responsible for the pregnancy of any girl. How clean the insemination and birth. For who could imagine the son of God squeezed by a woman's bloody uterine walls, his tiny wet head emerging slowly through her stretched cervix and vaginal opening as she cried out in pain? Had any of us asked, the ministers might have had to devise a more elaborate denial than that required by a virgin birth.

My only encounter with Mary *as a person* occurred too late in my life to inspire confidence: Colm Tóibín's fictional account *The Testament of Mary* gives more flesh and history to her than any biblical account. Tóibín's Mary feels rage at the opportunistic disciples who have built a story around Jesus's identity as the son of God. She feels grief at her son's death, fear for her own safety, and guilt for not staying with him when he died. As any mother would. The dream of her son coming back to life is just a dream. What really happened is unimaginable, Tóibín's Mary thinks, "and it is what really happened that I must face now in these months before I go into my grave or else everything that happened will become a sweet story that will grow poisonous as bright berries that hang low on trees."[14]

Colm, please write a novel about Eve.

The ministers did not always see the two-edged sword they waved over our heads. So busy learning how to please an invisible God, we innocent girls failed to notice how useful this instruction was. There were fathers to please, too, as well as our ministers, boyfriends, and other men who had authority over us. Instill the desire to please in a select population, and they become malleable and easy to manipulate. The process began with God and moved down the chain of command. We wanted to be loved by God, so we prayed and tried not to lie or let the boys touch us where they shouldn't. We wanted to be loved by our fathers, so we stayed quiet at the dinner table and did as we were told. Our mothers taught us that love meant not wanting anything for ourselves. To love was to please, to be the pleasing object of another's desire, to not have any desires of our own. To love, for a girl, was to kill her own eros—a Christian-style clitoridectomy.

So preoccupied with our desire to please, we did not know that the youth pastor who started our sex education classes was taking advantage of our trust. His talk flowed smooth as silk, and his power was sanctioned by God. We were brimming with youthful love and trust, and our innocence kept us pliant like our nimble bodies. When he asked us during one Saturday session to fantasize about a boy—as good as sinning, we had been taught—we felt the vague taste of violation in our mouths, something we would name only in the years to come. But we never thought to doubt him. Neither did we think to ask questions when he informed us of the proper position for sexual relations with our husbands (yes, only one position, and not the one you might think).

This trusted man became a statistic some twenty years later, a name in the local newspaper, thanks only to one young woman's courage in defying her own shame. The irony rankles: the pleasure of innocents fumbling under clothing evoked warnings of eternal burning, but men of God who knew what they were doing when they penetrated girls with the symbol of their God-given power were never the subject of sermons. No one thought to ask what the laws of eros were, if it had any, or if its anarchic nature—so vividly recalled in the Song of Solomon—might have saved us. Jesus rose from the dead, but eros remained crucified.

IF ONLY WE HAD READ
THE SONG OF SOLOMON

We would have learned of the adoration for the body that we discovered too many years later, after sloughing off the effects of moralism, the scales of shame and guilt that grew thick on our flesh. We might have thought our bodies less ugly, less repulsive if we had read

> Behold, you are beautiful, my love,
> behold, you are beautiful!
> Your eyes are doves
> behind your veil.
> Your hair is like a flock of goats,
> moving down the slopes of Gilead. . . .
> Your lips are like a scarlet thread,
> and your mouth is lovely. . . .
> You are all fair, my love;
> there is no flaw in you.

(Song of Sol. 4:1, 3, 7)

We would have learned of the good that comes from adoration, for we love a body, a particular body, luminous under the touch of our eyes. Desire for a body is desire for the pleasure of adoration and its effects: we coax the beloved to life with our lips and eyes and fingertips.

Had we read the Song of Solomon, we would have learned, too, of the yearning and elusiveness of love, its sickness, the thrill of opening even at the risk of rejection or loss:

> My beloved put his hand to the
> latch,
> and my heart was thrilled within me.
> I arose to open to my beloved,
> and my hands dripped with myrrh,
> my fingers with liquid myrrh,
> upon the handles of the bolt.
> I opened to my beloved,
> but my beloved had turned and gone.
> My soul failed me when he spoke.
> I sought him, but found him not;
> I called him, but he gave no
> answer. . . .
> I adjure you, O daughters of
> Jerusalem,
> if you find my beloved,
> that you tell him
> I am sick with love.

(5:4–6, 8)

Would we have recognized the sensuousness of these lines, overwhelmed as we were by the shame of our pleasure in the forbidden? What appeared to be as ordained as the movement of the earth around the sun now looks quite arbitrary. That sex should be the focus of a moral code seems as random as declaring that God is male or that Sunday should be a day of rest. But we were partial to arbitrary codes and worldviews. The same teacher who taught us the world was six thousand years old, as the Book of Genesis confirmed, also told us never to kiss before we were engaged to be married. I wonder that he never thought his instructions came too late.

BURNING

We were given two symbols to represent our humble condition before God: the docile, obedient sheep and the burning candle flame. We were taught to love a God who demanded everything of us, who asked for nothing less than our lives, our very beings, to be devoted to serving and pleasing him. Like a candle, we must burn for others—not only to light their way but also to expire eventually for their sake. A candle fulfills its purpose by burning up. We must give and give some more, until all is spent.

Like Jesus, whose sacrifice, we may discover too late, was ultimately useless. Too late, for love, suffering, and sacrifice were already sutured permanently in the ubiquitous image of the torn and bleeding body, stripped and humiliated in order to be loved by a most cruel and incomprehensible God and by centuries of human believers fleeing the nothingness of death.

There is no great leap to make from burning up for God to burning up for our fathers, for the men we love, or for our children. Think of Mrs. Ramsey in Virginia Woolf's novel *To the Lighthouse*, responding to her husband's demand for sympathy, "looking at the same time animated and alive as if all her energies were being fused into force, burning and illuminating," until "there was scarcely a shell of herself left for her to know herself by; all was so lavished and spent." Later, Mrs. Ramsey secretly wonders if she wishes "so instinctively to help, to give," in order to be needed and admired.[15] And, I would add, to be loved.

When all that is left is this shell or the remnants of a burnt candle, how can we experience love as something other than need? How can we experience ourselves as beloved in our own right rather than as a projection of another's fantasy? I may live through his life, see myself through his eyes (which might be glorious or devastating), experience his emotions, desires, and thoughts, while my own seem to hide, phantomlike, in my dreams.

Truly, we encounter the dark side of love when in our desire to be loved we lose precisely that which is best in us and maybe easiest to love. Yet how selfish it can seem to some of us—especially if we learned love from a mutilated body draped on a wooden cross—to keep something back for ourselves, to hold on to that which we should never give. And to do so we must love ourselves, believe ourselves lovable simply for being, rather than accepting the nothing that God (or someone else) has declared us to be without his grace. We burn and soon come to desire the burning. This erotic—indeed, orgasmic—madness of the medieval mystic Teresa of Ávila is evident in her vision of an angel's visit: "In his hands I saw a long golden spear. . . . With this he seemed to pierce my heart several times so that it penetrated to my entrails. When he drew it out, I thought he was drawing them out with it and he left me completely afire with a great love for God. The pain was so sharp that it made me utter several moans; and so excessive was the sweetness caused me by this intense pain that one can never wish to lose it."[16]

FIND THE CLITORIS

For how many men in the world does the clitoris remain undiscovered—literally or metaphorically—and for how many women, its pleasures undiscovered?

When I was in fifth grade, we girls were given a blue booklet with delicate sketches of young women on the cover, hair and skirts swirling together. "It's wonderful being a girl" was written in script that dipped and curved like the feminine body we longed to inhabit. We were informed of our power to create life and of the monthly death of lonely eggs along with their disappointed nests. It was 1972, and we glowed with our own mystery and waited for the magic to begin—to become beautiful and shapely like our mothers, to bleed discreetly and symbolically, to be desired and loved by the man who lived in our dreams.

No one told us about pleasure. We anticipated the bliss of warm lips and weddings but were unprepared for the pulse and throb in the unnamed regions of our bodies. We thought sex was intercourse, nothing more, nothing less, and assumed when the time came, we would know how to receive a man. For a girl to lose her virginity had nothing to do with her centers of pleasure. We were vessels, and the loss of virginity signified a rite of passage only: the loss of a dream of sexual pleasure that would be defined by us. No one ever mentioned the clitoris. Our discovery of its significance filled us with a confusion of delight and shame. The message was consistently mixed: our bodies were disgusting, our bodies would be beautiful to someone, our bodies should be repudiated, our bodies will produce life. But it was never about pleasure.

We were not prepared for the turn of suddenly legitimate desire—the psychological leap this fact required us to make on our wedding night. One signed paper to reverse the years of prohibition, anxiety, and guilt. One ceremony to erase the work of our imaginations with the full force of disappointment.

Because when we finally lost our virginity, we were shocked to discover it wasn't about us at all.

SHAME

When love is sanctioned as the desire of the subject to please the master and of the master to rule over the subject, however benevolently, fear enters into the equation. The ruler fears insubordination, the subject fears the ruler's anger. This is how we know the exchange is not one of love, for love does not admit fear.

It was 1979, and I was at a summer youth retreat. I could not go swimming because the boy who loved me did not want other boys lusting after me. The thought of displeasing him caused so much anxiety that I left my swimsuit behind so as to have an excuse, and when the boys tried to throw me in the lake fully clothed, I screamed and kicked until they left me alone, perplexed by the vehemence of my protests (and probably bruised). I did not question my boyfriend's motives, believing myself somehow to blame—not yet aware of the weight of Eve bearing down on me. Neither did I feel the incredulity I feel now at the memory of this anxiety—how strong was the shame over something within me equally desirable and dangerous and how strong my fear of a boy's anger. This shame and fear gave consent to his power over me—and in this consent we find one of the secrets of domination. Whether in an individual or a population, docility and obedience are easy to procure when one is born into inferiority and taught that salvation lies in pleasing one's superiors and fearing their displeasure. Easier still when the order to obey is sanctioned by religion. The initial justification is eventually forgotten, and the ordained simply becomes the normal.

Women who avert their gaze when facing men, cover their bodies to disguise their shapes, hide their alluring hair and mouths, or sacrifice desire on the altar of faith and marriage may have accepted the threat of their own erotic power. They may forget or deny that this threat is the origin of the limits imposed on their freedom, decreed by someone's God. What dangers lurk in obedience and the desire to please.

When we became young women we sat separate from our male peers in church to avoid distracting them from their worship. We were warned not to be too affectionate with them because touch meant something different to men, so our friendships rarely crossed the gender divide. For a long time, shame held us in check, preventing our curiosity about these unwritten rules—but not long enough to shake the effrontery I felt on travels in later years when Buddhist monks would not meet my gaze or Muslim men would not shake my hand. We may blame patriarchy for this predicament, but I was the one who felt at fault in these scenarios, and I was the one who would pay the price for any transgressions.

Shame marks like a stigma. It is through the eyes that we encounter one another as worthy. In this meeting, open face to open face, we acknowledge and affirm the other's existence; we respect this other self who faces us; we become aware of our mutual vulnerability, our shared exposure. But when the other forces us to lower our gaze and refuses to look into our eyes, we are negated, rendered invisible. It is a declaration of inequality or unworthiness. There is no justification for this shaming. The message is clear—the one who lowers her eyes is not of equal worth. No one knows this better than those who force women to cover their faces and look away.

How far into the body will the fear of women's erotic power invade? As of 2014, some 125 million girls and women in the world have had their genitals partially cut or completely removed. Sometime between infancy and the age of fifteen, girls are held down by their mothers and other women and cut by a traditional circumcisor, often without anesthesia or proper instruments. The clitoris and labia might be cut off completely, and the skin sewn together with the exception of a small hole for urination, menstruation, penetration, and childbirth. As a result, a woman can expect a lifetime of health risks: cysts, infections, infertility, difficult childbirths, multiple surgeries to widen or tighten the opening, or even death during the cutting.[17]

Not to mention a lifetime without sexual pleasure.

In the name of tradition, desire is prohibited to women. A girl who remains uncut will not be considered suitable as a wife, for it is believed her desires will lead her astray. In some communities, if a girl does not marry, the family will not receive the coveted dowry: a cow. Yes, *a cow for a clitoris.*

VULGAR LOVE

The arrogance of the man at the red pulpit is the arrogance of Paul is the arrogance of Plato. Arrogance is the gift of a male God, passed down through the generations from father to son. Christianity inherited the prejudices of Greek philosophy against the body, against woman, against the world of the here and now. Jesus, like Plato's Socrates, is man's link to transcendence—escape from the misery of body and world. In the New Testament, we find the same model of discipleship evident in Plato's texts—the celebration of a masculine lineage, the submissive adoration of the Father of philosophy or theology. Wisdom is passed down from father to son, a proliferation of motherless births. As always, the birth of ideas trumps the lowly birth of existence through the bloody cavity of the mother's body. Ideas without flesh are pristine. Clean virgin births.

Julia Kristeva writes that "all the philosophies of thought, from Plato down to Descartes, Kant, and Hegel, that have aimed to give the experience of love a strong hold on reality have pruned out of it what is disorderly in order to reduce it to an initiatory voyage drawn toward the supreme Good or the absolute Spirit."[18] There is nothing left of love if we prune out the disorderly, for in the realm of human relations there is only disorder. This does not mean we cannot understand or conceptualize these relations, but it means we must always attend to their context and comprehend the limits of our analyses. We have to live with the contradictions. What this refusal of disorder has meant for Western philosophy is an awkward, arid treatment of love, for it should be obvious that if we prune out the disorderly, we necessarily eliminate the body and the vast range of emotions at play in our intimate attachments. Philosophers have had to work diligently, and no doubt painfully, at this task.

What a powerful legacy with which we have been saddled, a combination of Western Christian and philosophical scripts regarding love that render ugly so much of what is beautiful about the physicality of love. But disorder inevitably creeps back into both philosophy and theology. Their gods are not as clever as we make them out to be. We must look for the "deviations," where passion refuses to submit to institution, if we want a different economy for erotic love than what religion and philosophy have bequeathed to us.

Four centuries before Paul's famous description of love to the Corinthian Church, Socrates and his clever friends sent the flute girl away in Plato's *Symposium* so the men could get down to the serious business of intellectualizing love, filled with wine and infatuated with their own thoughts. I wonder what the flute girl was thinking as she left the party. In Plato, we witness the birth of the exalted philosopher, rising like a phoenix from the ashes of corporeal life, with its unpredictability, impulsivity, and risk, to embrace a disembodied realm of ideals. Pure masculine lineage and earnest, homoerotic discipleship, the birth of beauty in thought, contempt for the vulgarity of woman—these are elements of the legacy: man's birthright. Exeunt the flute girls.

The wisdom of love is taught to Socrates by a woman, Diotima, but she is not actually present at the party. This is not our only example of a woman "whose wisdom, above all in love, is reported in her absence by a man," Luce Irigaray reminds us.[19] Women are supposed to be pleased with these crumbs from the master's table. Diotima, after all, is clearly a brilliant woman, capable of instructing the incomparable Socrates, who is hailed at the end of the party as the most noble and wisest of men, untroubled by harsh weather, hunger, or the ardent advances of the gorgeous Alcibiades. We should be grateful that Plato included her, but we do not even know if Diotima existed except as a literary device. She disturbs the text as an incongruous and sober representative of the defective sex. Imagined by Plato, obedient to his will, rising to the occasion of his benevolence in using a woman to convey the voice of a man.

What do we learn of love in the *Symposium*? That there is vulgar love—for women, for the "least intelligent partners"—when only sex is wanted; this is a diseased love that is ugly and disgraceful, crude and impulsive.[20] And there is noble love—for boys and for philosophical wisdom. Noble love comes from the heavenly goddess, Aphrodite, who, we might note, was not born of a woman. This love turns out to be obsessed with control and moderation—as older men mentor and instruct their young lovers, who seem to have little autonomy themselves and are expected to be submissive. In Aristophanes's speech—perhaps introduced as comic relief—we hear the timeless, happy love story of intimate attachments, one half searching for her other half. Once found, without reason, "the two are struck from their senses by love, by a sense of belonging to one another, and by desire, and they don't want to be separated from one another, not even for a moment."[21] It is not only sex that drives them but also something mysterious—an unnamed lack.

But love, for Plato, must be brought to its perfection, and this can happen only if we turn to the ideal, despising the "wild gaping" after a body in the pursuit of wisdom and justice. To love what is noblest, we have to reject the physical and look to the divine: the goal is to see Beauty itself, an idealized Beauty "not polluted by human flesh," of which a man's beauty can only partake in a shadowy sense. The philosopher (for it is always a philosopher) who ascends to this ideal will eventually give birth to "many gloriously beautiful ideas and theories, in unstinting love of wisdom."[22]

Before Plato arrives at this absolute end, he gives us a provocative detour in the person of Diotima. On the way to describing the ascent from physical to transcendent love, she tells us that the purpose of love is to give birth in beauty. For a moment, love is presented to us as movement—love in a state of becoming.[23] Love gives birth to children, but also to ideas and to a kind of renewal of oneself in relation to another. When someone makes contact with a beautiful person, says Diotima, "he conceives and gives birth to what he has been carrying inside him for ages."[24] In this way, love generates beauty and goodness. We can believe this to be true without agreeing with the rest of the dialogue, in which Plato recuperates this "becoming" into the hierarchy of "Forms"—an implausible theory celebrating ideals over actualities that even Platonists seem embarrassed about. Desire begins with bodies—we need not leave the body behind, as Plato tries to do.

We might call the *Symposium* a tribute to love—and it is surely that in places—but it is also a betrayal of love if we value the sense given to love by Diotima, that it is a gift one lover gives to another. Each draws out of the other the beauty and goodness that are there, carried within them as though their souls are pregnant. One lover is renewed in the presence of another. This is why we say to our lovers, "You have made me a better person." But Plato ultimately recovers his Platonism at the end of Diotima's speech, for the Beauty we must reach for "always *is* and neither comes to be nor passes away,"[25] and, wonder of wonders, it turns out to be Socrates who embodies this ideal. Unaffected by the material world or bodily constraints, a divine figure, the alpha male of philosophers, Socrates is the manifestation of Love itself, a divine Love, a God.

We do not know what the flute girls did after work. While the inebriated philosophers pontificated, life was being lived down there in the midst of vulgarity, uncertainty, risk, birth, and death—inescapably corporeal. No clean ideas there, no virgin births, no Platonic Forms to sully life.

AMBIVALENT PLEASURE

For fifteen years, Augustine of Hippo loved a woman of "low social standing"[26] whom he had to renounce in order to marry appropriately. He writes that he was deeply attached to "the woman with whom [he] habitually slept" and that to abandon her "cut and wounded" his heart, leaving "a trail of blood." But those were the years in which he was still "a slave of lust," as he puts it, still indulging in the "monstrous heats of black desires."[27] I think about what this Carthaginian girl might have had to say on the matter of love and desire for her philosopher-man. Was she his muse? Was it his passion for her that led to his definition of love as craving? Could she have known how fateful was Augustine's decision to crave the love of God rather than the love of a girl of low standing, how firmly it would suture Western philosophy and Christianity?

The depth of Augustine's feelings makes the *Confessions* delightful reading, although it dulls considerably as he progresses from the love of the flesh to the love of God. Writing in the last few years of the fourth century as a man in his forties reflecting back on his youth, he indulges in the most severe self-flagellation, reminding himself of his "carnal corruptions" so that he may love God and reject the "foulnesses" of his past. He describes in painful detail how he "ran wild in the shadowy jungle of erotic adventures," clouded by "muddy carnal concupiscence" and befogged by the "bubbling impulses of puberty." In the bathhouse one day, as the sixteen-year-old Augustine feels the "thorns of lust" rising above his head, his father is delighted to witness the stirring of his son's virility, exclaiming that he would soon be a grandfather. But looking back on those years as a man wracked with guilt, Augustine is miserable over his debauchery, over the years spent "rolling in the dung" of Babylonian streets with his miscreant friends.[28]

Hundreds of years later, Abelard, one of the most important French philosopher-theologians of the twelfth century, suffered as much spiritual agony as Augustine, with the addition of physical torture, for he was punished with castration for his amorous attentions to the intelligent and beautiful Héloise. As the story goes, he fell in love with Héloise while she was living under the care of her uncle Fulbert. Abelard was becoming a famous scholar, but when he met Héloise, philosophy lost its title as master of his passions. Predictably, he stopped working, started writing love poems and songs, and cleverly worked his way into Fulbert's favor so he could become Héloise's tutor. He wrote to his friend Philintus describing his new affliction: "I was a philosopher, yet this tyrant of the mind triumphed over all my wisdom; his darts were of greater force than all my reasonings, and with a sweet constraint he led me wherever he pleased."[29] The tyrant was eros.

But when Abelard and Héloise were discovered during one of their "more tender conversations," Fulbert banished Abelard from the house—not, however, before Héloise became pregnant. She did not want to get married—a mistress is free, whereas marriage is the "tomb of love," she told Abelard—but he persuaded her to marry in secret, give birth at his sister's house, and then live with the nuns at Argenteuil. The plan did not work. Uncle Fulbert would have his revenge and sent someone in the night to castrate Abelard in his bed. The jealous and shamed Abelard, in a move that he later admits to Philintus made him blush at his weakness (a rather understated response, we might think) forced Héloise to take her vows as a nun so that no other man could have her. He himself wandered for a time and then retired to a monastery. He confesses to Héloise in a later letter, "What a comfort I felt in seeing you shut up," satisfied that she would no longer return to the world.[30]

The letters between them after these tragic events convey all the familiar dualisms of emotion against reason, body against soul, and flawed human love against God's omnipotent love. Most prominent is the battle for control over the senses—over passionate, uncontrollable feelings for another human being. This struggle to triumph over matters of the heart causes great torment and ambivalence worthy of Augustine's confessions. In Héloise's letters, we find more pronounced ambivalence; she defies a faith that would condemn her extraordinary and virtuous love. This is what makes her letters splendid reading, a point to which I return later.

In Abelard's initial letter to Philintus, he is already clear about the hierarchy of the mind over the body, but the power of love allows him to ignore it. After his castration and separation from Héloise, however, he returns to philosophy, hoping to find "a remedy for his disgrace"—an asylum to "secure [him] from love." Abelard's most definitive statement on this point (one that characterizes much of the philosophical tradition): "What great advantages would philosophy give us over other men, if by studying it we could learn to govern our passions? What efforts, what relapses, what agitations do we undergo! And how long are we lost in this confusion, unable to exert our reason, to possess our souls, or to rule our affections?" Love is "a troublesome employment," and extravagant passions must be forgotten, says the wretched, castrated man. Reject pleasure.[31]

Abelard remains torn, however, between his heart and his head. He rails against love, on the one hand, chastising Héloise for making him miserable by being so loving and faithful and begging her to release him. "Allow me to be indifferent," he writes, "I envy their happiness who have never loved; how quiet and easy they are!" He is angry for his own weakness in writing to her and angry that love is such a deceptive tyrant. On the other hand, he admits he still loves Héloise. Although he tries to avoid her "as an enemy," his wandering heart eternally seeks her. The passion still lives in him—"the fire is only covered over with deceitful ashes, and cannot be extinguished but by extraordinary grace."[32]

The conflict that causes Abelard to say he both hates and loves Héloise is the result of serving two masters: religion leads to virtue, Héloise leads to love. And so he loves what he feels he "ought no longer to love." This deep split within Abelard necessitates the splitting of Héloise. The person he loves has to be separated from the passion he is supposed to detest, and because he must detest the passion, he must hate Héloise as well. She keeps him from God—as well as from philosophy and sanity. He accuses her of destroying his piety, and yet his passion is too great; he feels shame, a "perpetual strife between inclination and duty." He wants desperately to be saved from her—his salvation requires her withdrawal. Regard me no more, he begs her: "How happy shall I be if I thus lose you!"[33] Abelard was not the most sensitive of men.

But despite his hatred of the world, his despair of the "poison" or even "evil" of love, and despite his reasoning powers, Abelard confesses to Héloise, "My wandering heart still eternally seeks you, and is filled with anguish at having lost you."[34]

He should have listened to Héloise, not God, for she had an answer to this conflict: "When we love pleasures we love the living and not the dead."[35]

RIGOR MORTIS

Who among us would want to be loved by someone who says, "I *will* myself to love you?" Does this not imply that I will make myself love you because I really don't? An emotion can never be willed. This is what is most profound about human feeling—it cannot be coerced or legislated but always plays the part of the rebel, spontaneously bursting on the scene, unrehearsed, unruly. Emotions never lie.

We need to consider the unconscious motivations behind this boring repetition of prejudices in Western philosophy, prejudices that create entire catalogs of pathologies. The psychoanalysts have one explanation, the feminists another. But the prejudices persist, if more subtly, in milder forms.

Pathological is what the German philosopher Immanuel Kant calls love when it is not governed by the will—this is romantic love, which just happens to us. He distinguishes this kind of love from "practical love," an attitude of concern that we can will ourselves to have for others.[36] He does not stop there, though. We find out, as Martha Nussbaum puts it, that when we indulge pathological love, it "draws us away from the correct moral attitude, sapping and subverting it."[37] Romantic love is thus something of a threat. "Good" love, in contrast, is an act of will.

The philosopher's disdain for disorder in matters of love persists. Consider Jean-Luc Marion's opening to his philosophical investigation of love, *The Erotic Phenomenon*. He points out that philosophy today remains silent on love—for the better, he adds, because when philosophy speaks of love, it betrays love. In fact, he adds, "one would almost doubt whether philosophers experience love, if one didn't instead guess that they fear saying anything about it. And for good reason, for they know, better than anyone, that we no longer have the words to speak of it, nor the concepts to think about it, nor the strength to celebrate it."[38]

Why would philosophers know this *better than anyone*? It seems, rather, that philosophers are saying more about love now than ever. Whom does he include in this group, and would they be happy to be informed that they do not have the strength to celebrate love and, indeed, that they fear speaking of it? Marion believes the simple reason why philosophers cannot say anything about love is that they lack a concept for it. Who betrays love in this instance—those who write of love without a concept or Marion himself when he writes, "To declare 'I love you' sounds, in the best of cases, like an obscenity or a derision, to the point where, in polite society (that of the educated), no one dares *seriously* to utter such nonsense"?[39] If we no longer have the words to speak of love, and if philosophers know this better than anyone, I would argue the obverse: everyone else knows better than the philosophers that it is the concept that betrays love and that philosophers are afraid to say anything about love only because they prefer to take cover under concepts.

Marion's betrayal becomes apparent: "Of course, I am going to speak of that which I barely understand—the erotic phenomenon—starting from that which I know badly—my own amorous history. May it disappear most of the time within the rigor of the concept." And his final revelation—the ultimate derision of experience in the name of transcendence—comes in the conclusion of this text:

When God loves . . . he simply loves infinitely better than do we. He loves to perfection, without a fault, without an error, from beginning to end. He loves first and last. He loves like no one else. . . .

God precedes and transcends us, but first and above all in the
fact that he loves us infinitely better than we love, and than we
love him. God surpasses us as the best lover.[40]

Here is the idealization of love, motivated by a discomfort
with what we might "know badly." A transcendent view of love
that renders it idealized and ethereal, trivializes the extraordinary
capacity of the ordinary human individual to love by giving credit
only to God or some other metaphysical ideal. The stronger the
love and the more we perceive love to be inexplicable or irrational,
the harder we try to deny its humble origin in human emotion.
Love becomes sacred rather than embodied; we deny its fleshly
constitution and its vicissitudes: it can be weak or strong, accompanied by desire or protectiveness, mixed with anger, pain, or irritation. Our love can deepen or cease altogether. But if God is love,
then our own love is defective, a flimsy imitation. If love never
fails, as Paul told the Corinthians, if it "bears all things, believes
all things, hopes all things, endures all things" (I Cor. 13:4–7), then
we who fail to love without conditions can never hope to achieve
"true" love.

What a cold, arid world we are left with: the philosopher
and the Christian, desperate to shed the body and put faith in
a transcendent realm or spiritual being we cannot see or know,
declare "I love you" to be an obscenity and hide such nonsense
under the rigors of conceptual systems. Plato, enamored with
an ideal form of Beauty against which no human body can
compete. Abelard, tormented refugee of passion and desire.
Kant, prisoner of the will.

We live with these legacies and their ugly effects. Who hated
the body more, Christianity or philosophy? I moved from one
to the other, exchanged one set of fathers for another. Each was

intent on teaching me shame—for having the wrong body, the "nothing to be seen"[41] that nevertheless invited looking and possessing, the body-without-phallus that prevented a direct line to God or Reason. My access to truth and holiness had to be mediated through their male heirs, but at the price of the experience out of which all my thoughts originated and to which they returned.

Leave these men to their *best lovers*, I say, for who would want to bed the man who prefers the gods of his imagination over the warm body beside him? Let them bury their amorous histories under the rigor of the concept where blood drains and bodies stiffen. Let them have their rigor mortis.

PART II

LOVE

THE *WE*

THE sensations that come to mind when I think of my love for you rely on metaphors of air and water: I am inflated, inundated, floating, brimming, surging.

I swell with love for you. I surge toward you and experience the pleasure of desire and care—the siblings of love. My life becomes meaningful in a way it was not before; my days feel urgent in the awareness of the precarity of your life. I love you because you are there naked before me, suffering and surviving. Because you are loving me idiosyncratically, imperfectly, with ambivalence. Because you lay both your brokenness and your trust at my feet. Because I can. I love you in the stubborn belief that my love is omnipotent.

And there you are by some happy and most irrational coincidence loving me. Telling me with your mouth and eyes and hands that I am loved. I experience that irresistible pull into a shared existence, always aware of your proximity or distance. When I am separated from you by physical space, there is no corresponding geography in the world of our "we." Our thoughts are like threads that connect us—I think of what you would say about this new book in my hands or about the image on the wall before me, and I hear your laughter over something I just overheard. In this way, you are always present to me.

Love may intensify over time or fade away, but it is born in a moment of unnamable affinity. We call this "chemistry"— neuroscientists have one explanation and psychoanalysts another—but I prefer the term *affinity*, which brings us into the poetic. We do not love everyone. Something in another captivates us, draws us in—vulnerability exposed in an open face, something familiar yet different, the aura of a person that we cannot quite identify. A hand is opened, and we grasp it, an invitation extended, and we accept. We let ourselves into another life and our own alters irrevocably. In this way, our lives are inhabited by others, and even when we lose them, they remain lodged within us.

It is this initial affinity that becomes the foundation on which we build a world around a "we." Diotima's wisdom is sound. The beloved is before us, pregnant with beauty and goodness, and our love is a skilled midwife drawing out this nobility. This is your inestimable gift to me—to desire what is beautiful and lovable in me that I might feel something like the person you adore. I come to see myself through your eyes and hope that you will come to see yourself through mine, willingly accepting the risk of this intimate exchange for the sake of the we, the interworld arising between us.

I try to imagine what philosophy or religion might look like now if throughout history the confusion of human desire and affect, their origins in a mutable body, and the bittersweet nature of eros were celebrated rather than dismissed as irrational nonsense. So much of what is good and beautiful in life is irrational.

There is no reason in the scene before me—the blue of the sky and the deep clefts of a mountainside. There is no reason in how moved I am by the pine trees that line my path and stimulate my senses. There is no reason in the love I felt for you, no reason in the fact that I felt more loved by you than by those whose capacity for love exceeded your own and who loved without the torment it caused you to love and be loved by me.

HAPPY LOVE

I teach a course called "The Philosophy of Love and Sex" to undergraduate university students. They arrive with their baggage, I with mine, and I am never quite sure that we are on the same page, given that I come from a very different time and place—the dark ages of rural Mennonite Ontario, I like to tell them. Yet the source of their curiosity may be the same as mine. They want to understand their relationships and the emotions that wrench them this way and that, the demands of the social context in which these relationships occur, and the raw power of eros that grips them. They want to know if they love, how they should love, how they should be loved, and if they can be loved. At least, this is what I imagine they want; they may be there only because the title of my course beats out "Intermediate Logic."

Our myths of romantic love are thriving, maybe more so than ever before, given an intensified demand for perfection in beauty, sexual appeal, and love. I see very little evidence of skepticism from this group of students raised in a society grown used to divorce, atypical family configurations, sex education, HIV/AIDS and other sexually transmitted diseases—none of which I had any knowledge as a child. This should not surprise us. The media and our self-help and movie industries keep generating the same myth in excessive devotion: there is something called "true love," and it is bigger than us, it lasts forever—even beyond death—and our task is to find it. We will know, somehow, when we finally have it. But if that love ends, then we will think it was not true love and start the search all over again.

Each generation is as confused as the previous one when it comes to intimate relationships, and each struggles to manage a new combination of public discourses on love and sex while grappling with the legacies of the old. This process of negotiation leads to intriguing contradictions. In my classroom, I am surprised to find, for example, guilt over the objectification of women's bodies (that men's bodies could be sexualized for visual consumption has not been an issue) or over the experience of lust in general. *Promiscuity*, *sexual love*, *lust*—these terms are generally juxtaposed to *true love*, *romantic love*, and *unconditional love*. The moral distinction does not appear to hinge on whether suffering is caused: lust itself is to blame. When asked, most of my students have said that sex should be experienced with love, and yet they seem to think that our culture is obsessed with casual sex, while romantic love is on the wane. There are always objections to my interchangeable use of the terms *sexual love* and *romantic love*. An old association persists between sexual love as "only" lust (considered neither serious nor loving) and romantic love as virtuous, true love.

Students are now maturing in an academic climate of relativism, and they exit my course believing that love is whatever you think it is, despite any protestations on my part. Even after three months of exploring the ambiguities and contradictions of love, when I ask them what love is, they might speak in platitudes, reproducing endless variations of the theme of happy love, adding that it means something different for everyone. Given the striking parallels in the sentiments expressed by authors writing from 600 B.C.E. to 2013, I find this conclusion curious. But relativism seems to be the outcome of encountering the vicissitudes of love; my students mistake the paradoxes of love for its indefinability. We are rarely at ease with paradox, not even in institutions of higher learning.

Together we read and discuss some of the most passionate—and ambivalent—texts ever written about erotic love. Enter Sappho, Plato, Augustine, Shakespeare, Stendhal, Héloise, Abelard, Schopenhauer, de Beauvoir. With few exceptions, these thinkers betray a sense of bewilderment in the face of love's contradictions as well as awe for the sheer force of erotic experience and for its hold on the human heart. And they lament the loneliness and despair brought on by its loss. Sometimes my students believe that only God or metaphysics can lift us out of this mess or that we are saved from love's ambiguity by the myth of true love—unconditional, enduring, unfailing—and the laws of reason or science. They are unsettled reading Sappho on the bittersweet nature of eros and relieved reading Helen Fisher on the neuroscience of attraction.

The final characters of this performance: Gillian Rose and Hélène Cixous, undaunted by love's darkness, by the work of love without scripts. In a memoir written just before her death, Rose tells us that the language of happy love is a fantasy, that happy-love gurus would "condemn you to seek blissful, deathless, cosmic emptiness—the repose without the revel." It is the revel that Rose chooses, for without it "existence is robbed of its weight." She refuses an "edgeless" love that seeks to escape risk. We fail in love, we are forgiven, we are failed, and we must forgive. Again and again.[1]

In Cixous, as in Rose, we are surprised by disorienting, imaginative possibilities: love and intimacy beyond anything we might know. Love is not about knowing. The privileged term is *movement*: not a determined knowing, but an intimacy outside language, law, and reason. "What grips me is the *movement* of love," Cixous writes, an "aerial crossing of continents." With this, she leads us into an evocative analogy: "So is love the secret of acrobatics? It is trust, yes: the desire to cross over into the other. The acrobat's body is his soul. Is the crossing vertiginous? Like every crossing. Useless to contemplate or fathom what separates: the abyss is always invented by our fear. We leap and there is grace. Acrobats know: do not look at the separation. Have eyes, have bodies, only for there, for the other."[2]

I read these lovely lines to my students and ask them to imagine what love relationships might be—beyond Hollywood formulas. We flounder a little, finding substitutes for the scripts we already have, struggling for words to describe what is already overdetermined or as yet unnamed. We have to leap; we have to have eyes only for there, for what is on the other side. But to abandon our scripts is no easy task.

SWEET APPLE

Several centuries before Plato came into the world and rendered the love of bodies inferior to the love of absolutes, the lyrical poet Sappho wrote of the sensual power of erotic desire for a particular body. We have only fragments of her poems, but the lines that trail off, deferring completion and refusing resolution, seem a fitting way to describe love itself. Beginnings and endings are nebulous. Love relationships are never fully understood or resolved. Love itself comes in fragments, its narrative seamless only when we tell the story later, once hindsight has imposed linearity and pattern, preface and dénouement.

Sappho's poetry thrills as I read each line to my students, but it falls on ears already prejudiced against desire as a shallow forerunner of true love or, worse, as the very vulgar love Plato cautioned against. The students do not always share my enthusiasm; some even find her heartless because they have imbibed the idea that lust is temporary and shameful and has no part in enduring love, that it is, in fact, the antithesis of love. Many of them do not find any love at all in Sappho's fragments.

Sappho's eros has the power to unhinge us from everything that anchors us, everything that allows the illusion of control. It is like an "unmanageable creature" that stalks us; it melts limbs and shakes the mind; it burns.[3] Why separate desire from love? Do we not burn with longing for those we love intimately? Eros flares again and again—it arrives and departs. We are in its grip in the beginnings of love, but in later moments it may also surprise us, bringing with it a reminder of the intensity of our attachments. When we fear the loss of eros, it strikes again. We feel its power to move us unexpectedly, and we remain unable to manage its force.

Anne Carson attributes this power to the endless deferral of erotic passion, most apparent in Sappho's fragment 105a:

As a sweet apple turns red on a high branch,
high on the highest branch and the applepickers
    forgot—
well, no they didn't forget—were not able to reach
. . .[4]

The apple keeps receding as we reach for it; the pleasure of obtaining the fruit of our craving is continually deferred. First, it appears red and high in the tree. But then it recedes farther until it is on the highest branch, forgotten by the apple pickers. Even this does not satisfy—we discover in the last line that we were wrong again: they did not forget the apple on the highest branch; they were unable to reach it. Carson explains that "each line launches an impression that is at once modified, then launched again," and so "the apple begins to look farther and farther away." This poem "acts out the experience of eros," she concludes, beginning with an apple and ending in "infinite hunger." This is what Carson call "the erotic dilemma," the structure of desire that keeps us craving what is unattainable.[5] In this endless deferral, there is always an obstacle—a third term—inserted between the lover and the object of her love, that prevents her from possessing her heart's desire. The unreachable object remains hotly desired.

In Sappho's fragment 31, we witness this erotic dilemma in the trio present in the poem:

He seems to me equal to gods that man
who opposite you
sits and listens close
to your sweet speaking

and lovely laughing—oh it
puts the heart in my chest on wings
for when I look at you, a moment, then no speaking
is left in me

no: tongue breaks, and thin
fire is racing under skin
and in eyes no sight and drumming
fills ears

and cold sweat holds me and shaking
grips me all, greener than grass
I am and dead—or almost
I seem to me.[6]

Eros overwhelms us when we watch a stranger appreciate the
"sweet speaking" and "lovely laughing" of our beloved. It might
make us jealous, so hungry are we for the love of the lover. But
Carson does not believe that the poem is about jealousy. Nor does
she think it is simply a celebration of the beloved's beauty. Rather,
the fragment is about "the lover's mind in the act of construct-
ing desire for itself." This is not an ordinary love triangle, but the
three structural components of desire: the lover, the beloved, and
that which comes between them. They touch without touching;
they are joined while held apart. Without this intervening element, Carson argues, desire ends.[7]

Christian and Platonic arrogance wipe out the beauty of this
sensual life. As I write this, I am distracted by the presence of a
mother and infant close by and of her women friends who crowd
around to admire the baby. I am enchanted by this scene and by
the infant's response to his admirers. This is how the lucky ones
begin their lives, with the most sensual adoration, only occasionally bereft of touch. Long before any label is applied to an
experience of love, there is this living, breathing world of sensual
adoration. It is not even a question of knowing we are loved; we
simply feel it in the kisses and caresses from another, in the joy-
ous faces who gaze at us, loving every movement, every sign of
wonder and recognition. Why should we repudiate this adoration in our adult lives? Who does not long to be adored by someone, to be the object of another's desire and affection, to savor the
pleasure on their faces when we greet them?

One of Sappho's most sensual, lyrical fragments is surprisingly sanguine about what appears to be the end of a love affair. "I simply want to be dead," Sappho's lover laments before reluctantly leaving her, weeping over "how badly things have turned out." Sappho's lover is evidently devastated. But Sappho tells her, perhaps too cheerfully, that she should go and "rejoice," knowing she had been cherished. In case her lover is not consoled by this assurance, Sappho reminds her of the beauty and pleasure of their desire for one another. Remembrances of intimate moments follow, voluptuously conveyed—of garlands encircling the lover's soft throat, "crowns of violets and roses," the anointment of "sweet oil," and the delicate release of longing.[8] All the sumptuous particulars that Plato and the philosopher-theologians would vulgarize.

If we assume the speaker of the fragment's first line, "I simply want to be dead," is not Sappho but her jilted lover, Sappho might be saying, "My darling, we had it all, rejoice in the memories of love and move on." But her weeping lover wants to die. How are we to understand these lines—as another depiction of the erotic dilemma, our gift from eros, rife with ambivalence, paradox, confusion, and frustrated longing? It may sound callous to some ears, whereas others will appreciate the intensity and beauty of love as desire, never mind "how badly things have turned out." We do not know why Sappho's lover leaves her against her will, but there is no indication of blame or bitterness here. There is only weeping and suffering and Sappho's assurances that her lover was cherished, that she has reason to rejoice.

This may be unsettling: this cheerful acceptance—without resentment or despair—of a love that has cooled. But there is something admirable in this admission that love ended despite gratitude for the time of its flourishing. There is no reason to believe that Sappho's feelings were any less sincere than her lover's. They simply changed, as feelings tend to do. But it may also be the case that these two women had very different feelings toward each other to begin with: one woman shaken by eros, the other deeply attached to her lover, without whom death seemed a reasonable option.

Why would we need to judge one love as morally suspect? What is wrong with lust—with the brevity of this burst of desire that melts limbs and shakes us to the core?

INSATIABLE DEMAND FOR PRESENCE

Listen to Susan Sontag's notebook description of romantic love: "Being in love (l'amour fou ['*crazy love*']) a pathological variant of loving. Being in love = addiction, obsession, exclusion of others, insatiable demand for presence, paralysis of other interests and activities. A disease of love, a fever (therefore exalting)."[9]

The fever of crazy love also describes the attitude into which every infant is born: an insatiable demand for the presence of the mother to the exclusion of all others. The infant is mad with love, craving the solace and sustenance of her breasts with such an obsessive energy that any nudge on the infant's cheek will have her turning in anticipation, mouth open and searching.

We call this reflex "rooting," which might be an apt name for our relentless drive to experience once again the fever of such desire and intimacy. We crave an unconditional presence, even if that first unconditionality was only a fantasy. For we only dreamed that the mother would fulfill our every need and never leave us. We discovered much too late that she was only another human being, like us, with her own desires and disappointments.

And her face: archetype of all faces to come. The infant thrills to the contact of face on face, devouring with eyes wide open and unfocused the mother's skin and smile, swallowing voice and mouth together. Craving beyond craving, like the dead daughter of Toni Morrison's Sethe "looking for the join."[10]

Love is so intensely physical that the lines we draw between love and lust or love and desire are often arbitrary. It is impossible to tear the body away from the person we love. This is not to say that love and lust are never distinct. Surely we can experience lust without love—pure sexual desire for another's body, a stranger's body—and surely we can love without lust, even someone we once desired intensely. But there are intimate relationships in which love and lust are difficult to dissociate, when sexual desire for the other expands into a generalized desire—to give and receive pleasure that is not *only* genital. Bodies and psyches merge, move in unison; the loss of boundaries is an extravagant synchrony, "making" love in the truest sense of the word—creating a universe of pleasure out of skin and breath and conscious presence. Identities dissolve, like the features and lines of a face up close, blurred in the magnification of proximity. "The embrace of face by face is the true carnival of sex beyond gender," Gillian Rose writes,[11] a carnival beyond any simple demarcation between lust and love, beyond the borders of the self. For lust is also a carnival of mutual and extreme vulnerability. In the grip of this movement, we expose ourselves in ways we could not imagine in the ordinary light of day. We enter a place where we do not know where one body ends and another begins, where one ego bends in the presence of another.

Sontag refers to the fever of love as a pathological variant of love in the sense of excess. To be in love, in the grip of desire, is like a fever—"exalting," she adds parenthetically. We are invaded by a foreign force, Sappho's "sweetbitter unmanageable creature,"[12] and feel out of control. We crave what we do not have—like the sweet red apple high on the highest branch. Sometimes, the more it recedes, the more we crave it, and we shamelessly pursue the object of our desire. Augustine believed love is "a kind of craving,"—*appetitus*—a motion toward something desired for its own sake. He distinguished between *cupiditas* and *caritas*: the former a carnal love of the world in which we live, the latter a love of the world to come. In either of these forms of desire, when the beloved object is fully held or possessed, "the motion of love as desire comes to an end," and in this closing of the gap between lover and beloved happiness results.[13]

Not so, says Carson, interpreting Sappho's description of the erotic dilemma as highlighting precisely what gives us both delight and agony: "To be running breathlessly, but not yet arrived, is itself delightful, a suspended moment of living hope."[14]

But we do not only desire what is beyond our reach. There is a desire that is not a longing to possess. We also long to be close to what we love—Sontag's "insatiable demand for presence"—close to the beloved who also loves us, to our friends, to our favorite books, and even to our well-loved things. This is not a craving to possess objects in any superficial sense, but a longing for what is familiar to us, for what provides us with a sense of belonging and home.

This craving is not only to *be loved*, but also *to love*.

LOVE FOR THE LIVING

Love is never wrong. It is an emotion that above all affirms another's existence, and in this affirmation it is always physical and pleasurable. We do not love disembodied personalities, but a presence in the world, a face and hands, a voice. This seems too obvious to point out, and yet we continue to make moral distinctions that split love in two.

There is a striking difference in the letters between Héloise and Abelard that illustrates this point. Despite their mutual despair over the tragic outcome of their love, only one of them believes this love is wrong—even poisonous and evil. Héloise refuses to repent of her feelings for Abelard, and even her frequent expressions of doubt seem contrived, as though she must remind herself of what she *ought* to feel as a woman of God. But she will not renounce her passionate desire for Abelard because she cannot distinguish it from her love for him—the passion and the love are not morally separable.

How could she feel ashamed of love, how could she regret her love for Abelard? For when he is around, Héloise writes, "anything seems lovely to me, and nothing is ugly." It is not her feelings for God that inspire virtue, but her feelings for Abelard, and they are what makes her most fully human. In fact, despite some ambivalence from Héloise on this point, it is the convent, the symbol of her devotion to God, that threatens to undermine her humanity. She writes to Abelard: "You have not turned me to marble by changing my habit; my heart is not hardened by my imprisonment; I am still sensible to what has touched me."[15] And what touches Héloise, even if she protests that she loves Abelard the person, not merely the man, is their deep attachment—one in which the physical and the intellectual are intertwined. Her love is consistently expressed in physical terms. "How my eyes gloat over you!" she says, her greatest pleasure going to bed and thinking of him. Reason and faith fail to compensate for this engagement of the senses. "How will it be possible to keep thy reason at the sight of so lovable a man?" she muses, asking in obvious anguish: "Shall I never see you again?" Can I behold those brilliant eyes without recalling the tender glances or the mouth that "cannot be looked upon without desire"?[16]

Whereas Abelard wants only the serenity of his attachment to God and longs for release from his passion, Héloise will do anything to maintain their attachment, even risk her relation to God. The power of her attachment is stronger than the obligation of her veil. In her second letter, she is quite defiant on this point: "I am not penitent of the past," she declares, unapologetically devoted to Abelard though she alone is the slave of human desire among those wedded to God.[17]

Destructiveness is the only element of her love for Abelard that she regrets. Héloise blames herself for his castration. "I have not betrayed you," she writes, "but my constancy and love have been destructive to you. If I have committed a crime in loving you so constantly I cannot repent it."[18] She weeps for her lover, not for her sins, indulging in the pleasure of remembering past delights rather than abhorring her crimes.[19]

These letters show us how timeless and universal is the experience of intimate love. Despite changing social conditions that influence how our love relationships are conducted, the emotions engaged in intimate love seem remarkably constant. Arguments that place the beginning of romantic love as we know it in the modern era do not account for the resonance of these twelfth-century letters or, indeed, of Sappho's lines written some eighteen hundred years earlier, or, later, of Plato's remarkable tale of the spherical people whom the gods cut in half and who spend their lives searching for their other halves. We desire intimate attachments, and occasionally, inexplicably, we find someone to whom we attach ourselves so completely that life seems worth living only in the presence of this other person. The letters of Héloise and Abelard provide the kind of poignant tragedy we love to weep over, but they also lend insight into human attachment, at once pleasurable and painful. These attachments defy the norms, moral or otherwise, that we seek to impose on them.

In Héloise, we find a refusal to divide love into factions that must do battle, a testament to the claim that love—its pleasurable excess, its unapologetic attachment—is never wrong.

THE INFINITE PLASTICITY OF POSITION

The skin has its own memory. It spins fine stories on slow summer nights. Of motel rooms made for lust with their smell of old smoke and rusty tap water, their threadbare towels and telltale bedsprings. Of impromptu interludes witnessed by dusty books in the institutional silence. We were told that the spirit is willing and the flesh is weak—and passion is just a trickster. But our bodies offer up a different truth. Mouths open in supplication like baby birds without shame; hands mold like Pygmalion shaping his lovely Galatea, waiting for Venus to bring her to life. Desire feeds on desire, imagination on imagination. We forget self-consciousness in that place both foreign and familiar.

"Love-making is never simply pleasure," writes Gillian Rose; "sex manuals or feminist tracts which imply the infinite plasticity of position and pleasure, which counsel assertiveness, whether in bed or out, are dangerously destructive of imagination, of erotic and of spiritual ingenuity." Indeed, "the sexual exchange will be as complicated as the relationship in general—even more so." What I want is released inside your body and taken back into mine: "kiss, caress and penetration are the relation of the relation."[20]

You said you craved me constantly, like Ouroboros. Starved for my presence, drinking me with your eyes, eating me with your hands, sucking oxygen from my open mouth. And I craved your craving. What you wanted: not to be you. What I wanted: to save you from the you who wanted not to be you. A perfect fit.

L'AMOUR FOU

We "fall" in love. But Sontag suggests this is one "disease" we should hope to have often, which is less "mad" than falling in love only two or three times in one's life.[21]

We have long decided that enduring love is the best love and that falling in love is frivolous or shallow, especially if it is indulged for itself rather than as a forerunner to true love. We prize longevity in love to such an extent that we stigmatize those who have not experienced it, for whatever reason. It is never considered a matter of luck. The long-termers believe they overcame the problems that the short-termers failed to resolve, weathering the transition from shallow infatuation to deep commitment, which evidently the short-termers were unable to do—like failed marathoners or mountain climbers.

Listen to the philosopher M. C. Dillon, who complains of a contemporary malaise regarding erotic love. "We do not seem to know how to love well," he writes, a condition manifest in our inability to handle all the social ills around love relationships. He attributes this failure in part to the fact that in our time and place the "lovestyle" that prevails is romantic love, which "affirms the thrill of new love above all else." He defines romantic love as "the desire to appropriate an ideal, to possess perfection, to consummate a union with the beautiful object that betokens sheer pleasure." Quite simply, when we love romantically, we are in love with love, "with the ecstatic high that comes in the early phase of a romantic liaison." It is only the *experience* of love that is sought in this case, and the love object is only a means to an end. Unfortunately, bodies do not constitute the ideal that the romantic lover wants to possess, Dillon warns. Dissatisfaction ensues, again and again. We crave the ecstasy of new love, "cast ourselves into another whirlwind with the forlorn hope that this time it will not just add to the wreckage," and are inevitably disappointed again, only to make another desperate attempt.[22]

Dillon has more interesting things to say about what he calls "authentic love"—which eschews this fantasy of perfection and settles into the reality of another's existence—but I find his characterization of romantic love rather clichéd, like the caricature that is often presented by those who feel they have a claim to authentic love and have left behind forever the "lovestyle" of romantic desires. Dillon, in fact, refers to romantic love as adolescent; it is only a prelude to deeper, authentic love and therefore not really love at all because we cannot possibly love those we do not know.

What is wrong with loving love? I am compelled to ask. It may be true that what we call falling in love is generally a preliminary step to a more complicated, "deeper" love, but I would add that the hot beginnings of romantic encounters may not be preludes to anything—they are events in themselves, gifts from eros that come out of nowhere, like the surprise of a water balloon bursting in our hands as we catch it. A tiny explosion of intensity that leaves us more awake than we usually are, our senses at the ready—always bittersweet, as Sappho pointed out, because we live on the precarious ledge between having our desires returned or rebuffed. Our bodies react like exposed nerves to this madness, like electric wires, our minds alert. There is no need to compare the love we feel for someone we have loved intensely and for a long time to the feelings we have for someone we just met, whose character has presented itself in a preliminary sense only, uncomplicated as yet by the deeper operations of the self. What is at the heart of this distinction? Can we name it without making a value judgment, dismissing any notion of romantic love as vain idealization and desperation, its outcome inevitably disappointment or disaster?

At the affective level, the difference between falling in love and feeling what we like to call true love—or Dillon's "authentic love"—seems to hinge on desire. I hesitate to add the descriptor *sexual* because what is felt is a generalized desire, the expanded notion of eros that I have attempted to evoke. As Sontag and so many before her have suggested, this desire is like a fever, an insatiable craving for presence. It burns, as Sappho puts it. As we come to know a person more fully, of course these feelings are subdued by other feelings, not all of them positive.

But this does not mean that we love someone only after a certain amount of time has passed. A person's character unfolds over time and is also capable of radical change, sometimes slowly, other times suddenly. We love someone based on what we encounter at a specific point in time, just as we see a face from one angle first and then from another angle later; as this point moves, our perspectives shift. We are exposed to new facets of the person we love, facets that develop in relation to our own increasing exposure, and sometimes these revelations make us withdraw our love. There is no magical point in time at which we can say, "I now know this person and love her." We simplify the extraordinary range of possible feelings for someone if we reduce them to stages on a temporal continuum.

Consider the parallels with friendship. My closest friends are individuals for whom I felt an instant affinity and for whom I quickly felt affection and love. Some of these friendships are only a few years old. Falling in love is also characterized by this affinity—it is not strictly sexual desire we feel when we fall in love, if we are defining such desire as a genital drive. The initial feelings are affirmed with time as we continue to experience pleasure in another's company and in mutual, increasing vulnerability. The experience varies, of course. Some might experience their emotions more slowly or less intensely or have a more limited range of emotional expression; for them, falling in love might feel quite different. But in friendship or in sexual love, the pleasure consists in the "falling"—a free fall into naked vulnerability from the heights of protection and autonomy. The heady feeling of falling in love can arise at any time if we continue to feel the exquisite pleasure of another's presence. "Sweet love, renew thy force," writes Shakespeare; do not say that love's edge should be blunter than appetite, "which but to-day by feeding is allay'd, / To-morrow sharp'ned in his former might."[23]

Why would falling in love lead to malaise? We might say that malaise more aptly describes a culture that sanctions coupledom at great cost to personal integrity, autonomy, even mental health and physical safety. Both of these assessments of malaise assume a caricature that is hardly representative: the first, of romantic love as the search for a fantasy that is ultimately disappointed, and the second, of married love as stifling and dull. In either case, we should not assume that malaise can be generalized.

Commitment is hailed as the highest value in love, responsible for its longevity and authenticity. Those whose coupled worlds remain intact for a lifetime are celebrated for their exemplary love. We ask them for their secret, as though there is a formula we all might apply. Brief love is dismissed as an episode of frivolity— passion or lust, perhaps, but never true love. Enduring love is celebrated as virtue itself. But love is not commitment, although it might induce the desire to commit. Commitment may indeed be something to value, like hard work and honesty. We can commit ourselves to a relationship, to caring for another, to sharing life's burdens—and these are good and necessary features of human interaction—but we cannot commit ourselves to love anymore than we can commit ourselves to feeling hatred or fear. Emotions might be masked, but they cannot be changed at will. When we promise to love forever, we are instead promising to exist in proximity. Who would want to be loved if that love were a matter of will? To be married for life may have everything or nothing to do with love. It may be about a sense of duty, the need for security, or fear. It may be habit. Love must be given freely, outside the bounds of any law; otherwise it is not love, but something else.

We might do well to follow Shakespeare, who seems unperturbed by the range of erotic experience or the waxing and waning of love. He begins with human experience and ends there, as Allan Bloom points out, content to pass back and forth between the bawdy pleasures of lusty wenches and their eager suitors and the marriage of true minds, resisting moralism and the assessment of social ills.[24] Shakespeare shirks neither pleasure nor pain, for as much as love is a fever, a disease, a mad longing for what might ultimately disappoint ("For I have sworn thee fair, and thought thee bright, / Who art as black as hell, as dark as night"[25]), it is also a force that renders the beloved as lovely as a summer's day, immortalized in words.[26]

BEAUTIFICATION

When I think of romance, the most ordinary moments come to mind.

My beloved sits beside me, reading. His eyes flit rapidly across the page—he is greedy for words—and this scene has me enraptured. I burst into his peripheral vision, my lips on his cheek, loving him for the sheer movement of his eyes across a page.

The sound of my lover's voice has the same effect as the touch of his lips. The sensation is one of melting or falling from a great height. Heady vertigo as I feel my bones tremble.

I say his name. How I love to say his name, lips together, parting, tongue tapping the top of my mouth. As though love can flow in syllables off the tongue like the briefest of melodies.

What is romance in these moments but adoration for beauty—or, perhaps, adoration that beautifies? We observe beauty in one who is loved where others may not, but in the observation we are both passive and active, drinking in what we see, and beautifying with our very gaze.

There are two ways to read this beautification of the loved one. In the first reading, we call it idealization—when we idealize our lovers, we uphold the adage that love is blind. This seems to be Dillon's point of view. In the early throes of infatuation, all our fantasies of perfect love are projected onto the lover. This is the madness of love, its fever. The lover incarnates perfection, and we remain willfully blind to flaws until we discover that the beloved is far from ideal. When the blinders fall away at the first encounter with the "real" person, we may fall out of love.

There is another way to read this "blindness," for if we are closing our eyes to flaws, we are engaged in what Irving Singer calls "augmentation."[27] There are two approaches to understanding the nature of love, he believes, both having to do with valuation. We look for certain values in another, such as qualities or characteristics, and we create value in the person we love. It is the affirmative relation itself that "bestows" value on the beloved regardless of self-interest. In other words, we love and value the person, not her attributes, as we would value a home in which we have invested meaning and not the house itself for this or that feature. As Héloise remarks to Abelard, "True tenderness makes us separate the lover from all that is external to him, and setting aside his position, fortune or employments, consider him merely as himself."[28]

Singer details what augmentation of a loved one might comprise. He includes caring for the beloved's needs and interests, delighting in her achievements, encouraging independence while accepting her dependence, respecting her as a person, giving pleasure and sympathy. And missing her. In this way, lover and beloved create an affective universe, one of beauty and meaning. But Singer importantly stresses the function of loving rather than of being loved. Bestowing value gives birth to beauty as Plato's Diotima would put it, and in the process of creation the bestowal augments the giver as well as the receiver. In this way, Singer concludes, "even to say that the lover gives himself is somewhat misleading. Love need not be self-sacrificial."[29]

What Singer calls "bestowal," Stendhal calls "crystallization," which he explains is what happens to the bare branch of a tree that is dropped into the shaft of a salt mine and pulled out a few months later. "An infinity of diamonds" now coats the once ordinary branch, "dancing and dazzling," rendering it unrecognizable. The imagination works furiously here—one need only dream up perfections to find them in the beloved. The crystallization of a lover *is* her beauty, and it brings together "*all the fulfillments* of all the desires that he has successively formed about her."[30]

To those who would think cynically about the illusions of romantic love in its infancy, Stendhal responds that crystallization never ends—that is, *if* love survives the first harrowing phase of fear and doubt, both delicious and terrifying, and if the beloved affirms that love in return. Whenever we are not happy with our lovers, or when the intensity of new love wanes, crystallization takes over. It becomes "an *imaginary solution*"; we ensure perfections in our beloved with all the creative talent of our imaginations. Love transforms; "it acquires the new charm of absolute abandon, of unlimited trust," and becomes a "sweet routine that tempers life's troubles and lends its pleasures an entirely new interest."[31]

This is a wonderful description of the beauty that love creates in another. It is already there, latent perhaps, but coaxed out and cultivated by the lover. She is not delusional when she tells him he is the most desirable man she has ever met, even if all her friends think he is quite dull. He is not lying when he tells her she is brilliant and beautiful, even if no one else agrees. It is not merely that they see in one another what they want to see—otherwise, they might choose anyone—it is that love *affirms*, and the resulting pleasure is so great that we always want more of it.

Nothing I have said implies we can eliminate the risk of lying and deluded lovers who project a fantasy of whom they wish to love on the person standing before them. The higher the pedestal, the more disastrous the fall; the more twisted the lie, the more bitter the truth once known. But it hardly matters, as risks never amount to much of an obstacle in the pursuit of love. It seems we can't help it.

Love is not blind, then, but sees selectively. Facets of the beloved end up in the shadowy regions of our peripheral vision, willfully ignored, eventually forgotten. When the lover sees the beloved as beautiful, he becomes so. And who does not want to live as beautiful in the eyes of her lover?

PATHOLOGICAL LOVE

A man I once loved complained that he did not have the energy to say "I love you" all the time. He ended our relationship to devote his energy to writing a book. Or so he said. I found his perspective baffling, given that my own professions of love had the obverse effect on me. I thought love expanded with its flow; I thought that to give love increases its supply, like mother's milk the more her infant drinks. Where is the dilemma? In my attitude, exalting my lover, losing myself in my devotion to him? Or in his attitude, being unable to exalt, to lose himself in devotion to me? I thought of Plato, Augustine, Abelard, dismissing the women, those obstacles to enlightenment.

Unfortunately, both the unconscious and the social world interfere with Singer's lovely list of what constitutes the beautification of one's beloved. When we create ideals and elaborate norms to uphold them, we create pathologies. In "'Civilized' Sexual Morality and Modern Nervous Illness," Freud introduced us to an entire roster of pathologies—"neuroses," as he called them—when he described the effects of the social prescriptions for romantic love in early-twentieth-century Viennese bourgeois society. He argued persuasively that the submission of sexual impulses to the service of procreation caused all manner of nervous sufferings and perverse behaviors, from psychical impotence in men and frigidity in women to incestuous fixations and infidelities. And marriage, according to Freud, was no panacea.[32] Although he says little of love directly in this essay, his assessment of its social and psychological conditions introduces us to the often extreme contradictions of love relationships thanks to the norms and codes on which they are constructed.

Decades later in *The Second Sex*, Simone de Beauvoir diagnoses variants of pathological love among heterosexual, bourgeois women in mid-twentieth-century France. At the end of her analysis, she outlines what she believes are the conditions for an authentic love relationship, found in the "reciprocal recognition of two freedoms." Each lover would "experience himself as himself and as the other," de Beauvoir writes; "they would not mutilate themselves."[33] She means by this mutilation what occurs to women as a result of a patriarchal, socioeconomic order that bestows status and value on man, granting him the independence and autonomy to which woman has little access. Woman becomes narcissistic thanks to this predicament, her love for man idolatrous.

De Beauvoir heaps scorn on the woman who becomes both tyrant and slave through devotion to her lover; her idolatrous love creates a living hell for him. Love has, in fact, become her religion. The woman in love lives in her lover's universe; she wants to breathe in the air he has already inhaled. "She does not tire of saying—even if it is excessive—this delicious 'we.'" She is incapable of being self-sufficient, dreaming only of fusion with her sovereign subject, losing herself, body and soul, to the man she exalts.[34]

This woman is "mutilated" and therefore incapable of giving or receiving authentic love; she offers useless gifts, is trapped in a feminine universe, and is given "a sterile hell" for her ultimate salvation. As the inessential other, woman is forced to find meaning and substance in her attachment to man. This is not masochism, de Beauvoir insists, but "a dream of ecstatic union." There is no enjoyment of the pain of self-sacrifice, only woman's desire to appropriate the sovereignty or autonomy of the male subject. Through him, she will achieve the salvation she lacks. But if the woman in love abandons herself in order to save herself, de Beauvoir warns, she paradoxically "ends up totally disavowing herself." Her conclusion: love, for the moment, is a curse on woman.[35]

De Beauvoir's essay reads like an earlier version of contemporary references to "codependency"—a pathology named by the love gurus of our self-help industry. They warn against overinvestment in a loved one, dependency, and the lack of proper ego boundaries. Such warnings are commonly directed at women who "enable"; like de Beauvoir's mutilated woman, the "codependent" lives through her lover, takes responsibility for him, and thus risks excusing and enabling behaviors such as alcoholism or abuse. The antidote: setting boundaries, detaching from the beloved. The liberal self must be self-governing, only secondarily in relation to and minimally dependent on others; otherwise, one's capacity to love is crippled. Love yourself first, we are instructed, know who you are, learn to be alone before being with another. As though we are ever alone without always-already being in relation to others. We are all, in fact, codependent, in need of one another for our very survival. But there is a point to this warning, and it is as much about respect for one's person as it is about claiming reciprocal freedom.

The implication of this chapter of *The Second Sex* is that men are more capable of such authentic love, for they remain sovereign subjects; *they hold something back*. The woman they love is merely one value among others, and they want to integrate her into their existence, not submerge their entire existence into her. They do not abandon themselves like the woman in love.

The question of how I experience myself as a self *and* as an other is hardly straightforward. Our diagnoses of pathological or neurotic love attest to the confusion of human intimacy and our often conflicting needs for attachment and separation.

There is some truth to the designations *codependent love* and *idolatrous love*, thanks in part to the reality of the social conditions that foster these attitudes: patriarchy, capitalism, the heterosexual imperative, family values, and a flourishing romance industry combine to encourage us to make impossible demands on our lovers. The mysterious working of the unconscious leaps into the fray. In love relationships, it is not always apparent where one self ends and another begins. Our perspectives are not independent of each other; they slip into one another through shared language and a shared world—we live the beloved's life in intention.[36] We hold loved ones within us. Extract one significant love relationship, and we are different persons.

But where does the pathology begin? De Beauvoir's examples are specific to a particular time and place. Yet I read her depictions of the woman in love and glimpse a caricatured version of myself and of many women I know for whom love and care for another's needs are indissociable. Does this care not sometimes require the sacrifice of one's own needs?

THE INTERWORLD

Simone de Beauvoir misses the counterpart to woman's pathological love: the man in love, at risk of narcissism, in love with his sovereign self and fearful of woman's threat to his autonomy and freedom. He does not abandon himself, it is true, but sometimes this means he looms so large in self-importance that he fails to *see* her. Jean-Paul Sartre provides some insight.

In Sartre's view, because the other is free to perceive me in ways I cannot control, I feel the need to "glue" down her freedom. I want her to love me exclusively, to love me in all my uniqueness; I want her to choose *me*, to render me necessary, an absolute end. I am then no longer one "this" among other "thises," Sartre says; in fact, "I am the world" of my beloved. But without capturing her freedom and therefore eliminating the risk of her negative determinations of me, I cannot be saved from instrumentality. Sartre sums up the conundrum: "[one] wants to be loved by a freedom but demands that this freedom as freedom should no longer be free."[37]

This explains a great deal: everything from the love of a demanding God to the love of the lover who says, "I am the world! So attend to my needs but ask for nothing in return."

The desire to crush the freedom of one's beloved is no doubt evidence of pronounced narcissism rather than love, bolstered by the fear of exposure, of one's own fragility. In Sartre, we find the precursor to Jean-Luc Marion's pronounced concern with the question "Does anybody love me?"—although Marion insists that this concern is not about the certainty of being. For Sartre, there is demand and need for recognition, affirmation, justification—I am because I am loved—but the emphasis is solely on how the other can reflect me, on what the other can give to me or do for me, or, conversely, on what the other might take from me if I give her too much power. This explanation assumes a self–other dichotomy in which the essential and the inessential, the self and the other, are perpetually engaged in a zero-sum game.

There is another way to view the dynamic, however. To understand the self in love, why not begin with the act of loving rather than with being loved? Rather than "Does anybody love me?" why not ask, "*Do I love?*" and reconsider de Beauvoir's point— that I must experience myself as a self *and* an other—from the perspective of the loving self? This point of view shifts the focus from the terms of autonomy, from withholding and protecting, to the terms of vulnerability, to openness and risk in the movement of love. For there is no love without abandoning one's position and, like Cixous's acrobat, "crossing" over an abyss. In one motion, we abandon ourselves and reach for the other. There are limits to this abandonment, we must not forget; it is not an absolute abandonment of the self for the other, not a *substitution*.

In taking this leap, we may *find*—rather than relinquish— our freedom in loving another. This is the freedom of creation, of entering into an "undivided situation," as Maurice Merleau-Ponty aptly puts it. Our selves do not unfold in solitary confinement. I perceive another, and around her "a vortex forms, towards which my world is drawn and, so to speak, sucked in: to this extent, it is no longer merely mine."[38] The other invites me in; I respond to this call to be drawn in and in doing so create an unprecedented connection, an "interworld." The selves within this interworld shift, accommodate, move together, and then move apart in a constant—if inconsistent and unpredictable— dance. The intensity of the love varies, as does the degree of the boundedness of the world the lovers create, for many reasons or none at all. Any affect may be completely beyond reason or at most an expression of whatever retroactive reasons we might find in unconscious compulsions.

Love is the emotional force that propels us outside of ourselves to experience in some sensual, affective way life on the other side of a body. This is the undivided situation: "One is not what he would be without that love," says Merleau-Ponty; "the perspectives remain separate—and yet they overlap," and in this process the experience of another is necessarily alienating "in the sense that it tears me away from my lone self and creates instead a mixture of myself and the other."[39]

To love is not, then, to crush the beloved's freedom in order to stave off the threat she poses. When we love, we find our freedom "precisely in the act of loving, and not in a vain autonomy."[40] This is not the freedom to do as we please regardless of others' interests; it is freedom from ourselves. Love saves us from a barren narcissism. Just as a conversation frees us from our lonely musings to draw from us thoughts we did not know we had,[41] so love frees us from ourselves and propels us into worlds of affect, sensuosity, and generosity that we never knew before we loved.

The lone self does not entirely disappear in this interworld created by two—it retreats, altered by the relation with another. There is still a self, although it is never unaltered by another self— never an isolated, autonomous, or sovereign self. We know this because no one can live our lives for us. The one who attempts to live another's experience through total blind sacrifice, like de Beauvoir's woman in love, is nevertheless embarked on her own project. We might think this sacrifice is altruism, Merleau-Ponty says, but "this interworld is still a project of mine, and it would be hypocritical to pretend that I seek the welfare of another as *if it were mine*, since this very attachment to another's interest still has its source in me."[42]

There is a fluid boundary between lovers.[43] This is what is most pleasurable and at the same time most terrifying and painful about love. We are both bound and unbound through love, says Gillian Rose; this is the essence of the love relation, for the unbounded soul is as "mad" as the soul with "cemented boundaries." We have to accept both others' and our own boundaries while remaining vulnerable or "woundable." In this way, we grow in "love-ability."[44]

THE GIFT

I know the edge of love because I am a mere spectator to your pain. I creep up to the edge as much as possible, but I can feel your pain only metaphorically.[45] My body feels an echo of your suffering, but mine is an intentional suffering. I do not suffer as you do. I feel what is not there in actuality, as you feel your phantom pains. My anguish wrenches me from myself. I will the end of your suffering, but my love cannot collapse this abyss of skin and bone and pain between us. I can only transcend myself through empathy, like Virginia Woolf's Mrs. Ramsay, pouring a rain of energy "burning and illuminating" into the room where you lie.[46]

At the side of a hospital bed, I suspend my self, my needs and preoccupations, and become wholly consumed by love for the sufferer. I become, in fact, like de Beauvoir's scorned woman— breathing in the air you expel, oblivious to all but the "delicious 'we.'" When we feel pain in our bodies, it can dull our senses to the world; we turn inward, and the pain encases us like a cocoon. Love for the other in pain can do much the same. I do not look at the separation; I have eyes, a body, "only for there, for the other," to return to Cixous's acrobat analogy.[47]

But it is still me who looks at you from where I stand. It is still me also needing, craving, existing in our interworld as well as beyond it. Your version of autonomy is alien to me. You call it dignity. *My body, my choice*, you say to me as you continue to ignore the effects of *your body, your choice*, on me. And so we both protect your autonomy and dignity but ignore mine. What kind of autonomy demands the sacrifice of another's? Only the infant legitimately proclaims "I am the world!" and fails to acknowledge the mother's autonomy, for the infant lives in an undifferentiated world, incapable of looking back on herself through another's eyes. The entire project of childhood can be summed in the necessity of correcting this incapacity.

I always thought love is a gift, not a sacrifice. I gave to you what was good in me in the ardent wish to make your life better, but it was no sacrifice of self. Not, that is, until your autonomy became a monstrous assertion of infantile need. The love of another is never a right, nothing deserved or owed to us. It is a gift in the truest sense of the word, its recipients the arbitrary beneficiaries of luck. Love is also a gift to its giver—but only if in giving it she is not stripped of all that enables her to love.

"VOLO UT SIS"

At the end of Toni Morrison's novel *Beloved*, Paul D, his head hurting from all the things he feels for Sethe, recalls a friend's description of his lover: "She is a friend of my mind. She gather me, man. The pieces I am, she gather them and give them back to me in all the right order. It's good, you know, when you got a woman who is a friend of your mind."[48]

This is how we know ourselves—through those who gather us together with their love, all our tangled bits and trailing parts, and offer us back to ourselves in the right order. Our vulnerability is held gingerly in the palm of a warm hand until it no longer trembles—this is the hand of the friend who loves me enough to tell me who I am, the friend of my mind.

When we love, we save ourselves and others from the prison of invulnerability. In love, I am free to will you to be. Who speaks of the lover's voracious need to love? Who captures the exquisite delight I take in loving a person, a particular body: the lines that fan out from *your* eyes, *your* neck with its downy hair, *your* gestur-ing hands, and *your* voice that provokes a rush of feeling like no other? Who has written of the pleasure I experience in abandon-ing myself to the giving of love rather than its receipt? To listen in the dead of night to your fear and your heartbeat? To absorb your anguish, bind your wounds, tell you how immeasurably lovable you are? Who has acknowledged the generosity of the permission to love with abandon?

We leap, and there is grace. Here we find something akin to the "supreme and unsurpassed affirmation" highlighted in the expression "volo ut sis." "This mere existence," Hannah Arendt writes, "all that which is mysteriously given us by birth and which includes the shape of our bodies and the talents of our minds, can be adequately dealt with only by the unpredictable hazards of friendship and sympathy, or by the great and incalculable grace of love, which says with Augustine, '*Volo ut sis* (I want you to be),' without being able to give any particular reason for such supreme and unsurpassable affirmation."[49]

We love a person who is more than the sum of her parts, a bare, embodied existence, not qualities or characteristics; in love, we form attachments that deepen over time through the slow nurturing of a world, a history, through mutual care and survival. In this love, psyche and soma are in profound confusion—we do not love one without the other. And the self becomes a self in this love, for we are not self-sufficient and crave something beyond ourselves. "Strictly speaking, he who does not love or desire is a nobody."[50]

If love is expressed as "volo ut sis," it must remain an open ges-ture toward another rather than a flinching away, an outstretched hand that wills the other to be—essentially to be free—and that accepts the risk and the gift of love together. It is my vulnerability in the encounter with another that enables me to love, for when I am exposed to the other's perception of me, I experience myself as both a self and an other. This is the antidote to narcissism and its impenetrable barriers. I can attempt to see myself as he sees me, but because I am also a self, I must withstand his anger or disappointment. In this way, I protect my capacity to love. I am not keeping another at bay for fear of his power to determine me; I am refusing to let him take from me the essential condition for me to love—my open hand. At the same time, my fearlessness in the exposure to love allows the lover to flourish, to live his own life as best he can. We thus abandon the language of liberal autonomy and throw out our scripts for authentic love. We acknowledge that we love the imperfect and that we love them imperfectly. Not even God can do this; we imagine he loves the imperfect, but we do not allow him to love imperfectly. Imperfect love is uniquely human.

PART III

LIMITS

AMPUTATION

THE surgeon made a mark where I would run my hand, loving the shape, the soft hair and the muscle, the bone and skin of you. A black X made with what looked like a common magic marker. There would be no mistake. I'll not forget the image: that surgeon, having had his morning coffee and checked his schedule on a muggy day in July, marked an X below the knee where he would perform a routine amputation. He would save a life and alter it completely in one morning between coffee and lunch.

In the halls of hospital wards, we find love stripped down to the bone. Love is there in the recovery room, in the rhythm of my fingers tracing the path of your pain. There in the waiting room, the air rank with anxiety as we who wait for news shift in our chairs, mechanically sip weak coffee, and watch the clock. This love is potent and sharp, all the accumulated misunderstandings, irritations, and wounds—the rise and fall of any living, breathing love—expelled like bad air, like so much banality in the face of death. The remainder: love boiled down to its purest form, its sole object the suffering body. Merciful, like the morphine that dulls your eyes.

I was the eye of love's storm, willing the destruction of your suffering with iron determination. But my will, in the end, betrayed me. This was the source of my own pain: to caress your face, smooth your hair, bathe your body, yet remain unable to suffer in your place.

Now I know: to love you was not to suffer in your place and so to alleviate your pain. There is no substitution—this is the limit of love. I could not be your leg for you. I could not be your crutches. I could not absorb your pain to free you of it. I could not be your will to live or your excuse to live badly. I could only love you beside you, fighting against the limits of what my love could do for you.

In the end, we can live only our own lives in the most bearable way possible. I could love you only by letting you be, for this is love's "incalculable grace" and its singular power: my desire to let you be—Augustine's "volo ut sis"—my unsurpassable and inexplicable affirmation of you.[1] No one can love or be loved without this *wanting the other to be*. Without it, we arrive at love's limit, at the mark of an X, the point at which we must choose life.

For there is another kind of amputation. My terrified lover begs with one hand and cuts furiously with the other. Do not abandon me but leave me now. Love me unconditionally, but if you do, I will destroy you. Be my leg for me, and I will cut you off without mercy. Try to see for me, and I will gouge out your eyes so we are blind together.

I want to let you be, but you need to let me be. This might be the only reciprocity that love demands of us.

"YOU MADE MY LIFE BETTER"

In Lorna Crozier's memoir, *Small Beneath the Sky*, there is a stunning moment that disrupts the symmetry of our liberal ideals of romantic love. Crozier describes an intimate family scene: her mother, standing at the edge of a salty, alkali lake in Saskatchewan, scatters her husband's ashes to the wind and says, "You made my life better." She said this to a man whose drinking habits kept the family in poverty. He was not an abusive drunk but an embarrassing one, we read, whose disgraceful behavior required a cover-up of secrets and lies; his drinking "had to be carried invisibly, like a terrible disease that had no name." This love is hardly "proper" according to our social measures. Of her mother's parting words to her father, Crozier writes, "It was one of the most shocking things I'd ever heard. Only she knew what he had given her; only she could offer him those final words of love and praise."[2]

There is something quite striking in this story. Here we have an honest appraisal of love for an imperfect being who made a woman's life hell in one moment and worth living in another. At the same time, it is a grateful acknowledgment of the gift of his love, the love of a selfish man with little affection for his children, but love no less. How this gesture flies in the face of much of what we believe to be true of love: that it searches for perfection or that it is perfection itself, and if such perfection is never achieved, then we know not love—or only a poor imitation. We may find, paradoxically it seems, that our deepest love was for the most flawed person or that we received the greatest gifts from someone who never knew what was given.

Someone might object, invoking the suffering an alcoholic can cause a family. I am not denying this suffering, quite evident in

Crozier's memoir; I am throwing into question our assumption that love and suffering are antithetical. The one who causes suffering is still capable of love, and the one who suffers is not in love with the suffering.

I return to another memoir. *Love's Work: A Reckoning with Life*, written by the British philosopher Gillian Rose while she was dying of cancer at the age of forty-eight, is filled with stories of love and suffering. Rose admits that she is "highly qualified in unhappy love affairs" but refuses to find solace in an idealized version of love as exchanged between two individuals equal in their capacity for love.[3] The experience of love tells us it is not conditional on an authentic or mature relationship; the distinction Rose makes evident between an intimate relationship and love itself means that failed relationships do not necessitate failed love. Love itself is the expression of *this* body toward *that* body— a particular creative act, like a work of art.

In *Love's Work*, we encounter characters who live in the density of imperfection, dying of AIDS or wasted by other diseases, loving or lusting with varying degrees of success. There is Edna, ninety-three years old, adorned with a false nose and working as a secretary to Gary, who also suffers from a debilitating disease. Rose speculates that Edna survived a cancer diagnosis at the age of sixteen "because she has lived sceptically" (9). Edna has not lived a perfect life, Rose explains: "She has not been *exceptional*. She has not loved herself or others unconditionally. She has been able to go on getting it all more or less wrong, more or less all the time" (9).

We are introduced to Rose's own paternal grandmother, whose favorite curse to her husband was to call him a bandit in Yiddish, as if to say, "You are incorrigible, but I must love you" (18). We meet Yvette, whom Rose describes as "predator not prey," sixty-five years old and the lover of three men concurrently (24).

Yvette was "completely devoted to pleasure without guilt," Rose tells us, "affirming the validity of every tortuous and torturing desire" (28), celebrating "lustful love" (30), shamelessly pursuing men only to dismiss them, until the very end of her life. Reflecting on Yvette's funeral, Rose concludes: what Yvette gave to her friends, to people young and old, was "her courage to face the terrors of desire in themselves" (32).

And there is Rose herself, whose unhappy love affairs begin with a girl's love for Roy Rogers (61) and reach their apotheosis in her passionate love for Father Patrick, the loss of which is particularly wrenching—a loss "for which there is no consolation," not even writing (59–60).

In these tales of unhappy life and love, Rose conveys a passion for living that is indistinguishable from a passion for loving. Her favored term for this attitude is *revel*—without it, "existence is robbed of its weight," and love becomes "edgeless," without risk (105–106). Rose thumbs her nose here at liberal scripts with their language of happy love, for happy love is a fantasy, she says, and happy-love gurus would condemn us "to seek blissful, deathless, cosmic emptiness—the repose without the revel" (106). It is a fantasy shared by the proponents of alternative healing, she points out, whose injunction is this same edgeless or exceptional, unconditional love. They effectively promise eternal life but only by effacing the difficulty of life and love, for, they say, those with unhappy lives "are predestined to eternal damnation" (105). But it is precisely in these unhappy lives that we actually live, Rose insists, where we fail and forgive (105). Rather than equality and reciprocity, Rose highlights the vulnerability of the self as a condition for love. There is only mercy in love relationships—no democracy. Even if I am bound to get love wrong all the time, Rose declares, I will not stop "wooing," for that is "*love's work*" (106, emphasis in original).

Both of these memoirs push us to think beyond the liberal platitudes of a culture besotted with the belief that all of us can find a soul mate who is our equal, who buried his or her childhood baggage long ago and comes to us pure of heart, emotionally mature, psychologically whole, happy and eager to fulfill our every need forever (and that without this we are doomed to being alone with our flawed and unhappy selves, also forever). Crozier and Rose depict love as it is limited by the human condition—*as love is actually lived*. As a powerful affect, love may be unlimited in itself—there is no end to how much love we can feel—but it is experienced under certain conditions, limited by our individual capacities for love. The only unconditionality of love is the acknowledgement of its conditionality, Rose says (105). And although there is no democracy in love relationships, there is mercy—no perfect equality or reciprocity, but vulnerability. This is love's condition. We are able to love because we are vulnerable. If we lose our ability to be vulnerable in our encounters with others—to accept this risk and conditionality—we lose our capacity to love, for love always requires an openness to the other.

Perhaps what Crozier's father gave to her mother was not only his own limited love but also the opportunity for her to love with abandon, to love brokenness and disease. We could not in any sense call this an equal, reciprocal love if we are measuring love only in terms of its give and take in a relationship. Some, in fact, might want to call Crozier's mother masochistic. But if we consider *the love itself*, there should be no surprise that he made her life better, no surprise that he gave her something. Love is not an equal exchange or a level playing field, but rather a gift that bestows meaning and pleasure on the one who gives it. Its effects on the recipient are variable and unforeseen. Love is never a matter of measure or calculation between the giver and the receiver. No one else can measure the love that we receive from another, not even the one who gives it.

However limited this man's love and gifts were, he did not take from his wife what enabled her to love. The conditions for loving are dependent not on the relationship as reciprocal or equal but on one's ability to remain vulnerable enough to love. It is not our commonly diagnosed pathologies that erode our capacity to love—our imperfections, our struggles, and the crutches we reach for are not in themselves responsible for this erosion. On the contrary, our vulnerability to these conditions open us not only to risk but also to eros. In the encounter with another's raw vulnerability, with his exposed wounds and sensibilities, we open ourselves to the transforming power of love. We love more intensely, more tenderly. We love without fearing the risk to ourselves. There is power in this vulnerability.

The limit to love can be articulated as the point at which the lover harms or destroys our capacity to love. At issue is not the limit of giving, but limitless *taking*. Letting the other be, that inexplicable affirmation of the other, does not mean letting the other destroy us.[4]

ON THE QUESTION OF WORTH

Some of us love wounded things. When I was a girl, I played in old barns overrun with cats and was a magnet for stray dogs in the neighborhood, generally mangy and dim-witted. I loved them shamelessly, fattened them on dinner scraps and dry dog food, then mourned their inevitable deaths by farm machinery, passing cars, or once, I suspected, a puddle of pesticides. One of these strays bit her own puppy nearly clean through her tender belly, for reasons I could not fathom, and despite my fierce determination that the puppy should live, he died. Another canine companion was hit by a car and lay dead in a ditch for at least a few days, in plain view of my passing school bus. I stared at his final death face twice a day—teeth exposed in a grimace and neck impossibly twisted—until someone mercifully buried him, and I cried more for him than for my recently deceased grandmother, who I reasoned was enjoying heaven, unlike my poor dog.

Love defies logic, and this is probably a good thing, for otherwise we all would love the same person, the one who is judged to be most worthy of love. No one would love those who need it most, who crave excessive affirmations of love to compensate for deprivation, and whose need is a powerful seduction. It is not necessarily courage or altruism that draws us to the hungry, but the happiness of meeting this need.

Love is not a matter of worth; we choose a love object—or it might seem like a love object chooses us—and there is nothing to be explained in this event.

MY BEST THING

I had a recurring dream. A child was drowning; sometimes it was a baby. I screamed for help, but no sound came out of my mouth. I plunged my arms into the churning water, but the infant eluded me and sank under the surface. Panic would rouse me from this dream, arms still flailing in the empty air around the bed, still mute, as though my mouth were filled with sawdust. My relief on realizing it was a dream did nothing to alleviate the despair over my failure.

I thought the baby was you, carried away by the currents of your unconscious, your diseased body dragging you down. Those were fitful nights of vigilance after the first seizure I witnessed, after the hours in emergency waiting rooms, your body trembling with fever. But my mother said to me later, "The drowning baby was you."

I bore the weight of your sorrow, washed away the vomit and the blood, wiped the sweat from your skin, filled the gaping mouth of your need. It wasn't that. It was never that. It was the weight of your rage that defeated me. I could never pay for the sins of others, the black hole of their debt to you. I could never compensate for your shame or accept the burden of blame for what you had done. I stood at the brink of this impending disaster and chose life—not only mine but also yours. Love is not a cure for disease when it is refused, vomited up with each dose.

Need and rage in equal measure—rage against the need—like the infant fighting with the mother's breast, frustrated and furious and wanting more all at the same time. I failed to notice the depletion, *refused* to notice that something was being stolen from me. Slowly, like air siphoned out of lungs until they clench and risk collapse. And I refused to admit that my stubborn love was not helping, its irresistible impulse—to put together what is broken—the wrong treatment. For the burn victim, any touch, however tender, causes intolerable pain.

This was my hubris: I believed my love would endure, for love bears all things—it knows not failure. I believed my love was invincible—it could heal any wound, meet any need. But you, like the child in my dream, would not be saved, defying love's impulse.

To meet another's need for love and care permits us to feel necessary in a world that never stops throwing our insignificance in our face. Until the day we discover that such need can consume us, like a black vortex that sucks unsuspecting victims into its whirling mass. There are things we cannot and should not endure. I could not let you take from me what was taken from you—my capacity to trust, to be vulnerable enough to love without torment.

"It's what you can bear," Laura Brown says in *The Hours*.[5] You have to choose life when the only other option is to sacrifice yourself completely for another.

PEELED SKIN

We do not always know what we can bear when too much has been asked of us or taken from us. In his novel *Be My Knife*, David Grossman tells a love story through an exchange of letters between a middle-aged man and a woman he does not know but sees briefly at a school reunion. Both are married to others. In his first letter, Yair tells Miriam his heart's desire is to tell her about himself in writing—there will be no meetings in person or any interference in one another's lives. He wants to give her things he can't give to anyone else—"things I didn't think could be given," he writes to Miriam.[6] The vulnerability of Yair's desire is so naked it unsettles the reader.

Grossman approaches love in this story fearlessly. He confronts what our myths about love seek to erase—the pain of exposing ourselves to another and taking the risk that we will be knifed, figuratively speaking. But here, in the force of Yair's insatiable need to be vulnerable to Miriam, to be known in the most banal as well as the most profound sense, Grossman twists the knife metaphorically, so that we see it not only as a potential weapon but also as an instrument of the most tender yet powerful love, the kind of love that strips away our defenses against intimacy.

This stunning passage can be found a few pages into the novel: "I wish that two total strangers could overcome strangeness itself, the mighty, ingrained principle of foreignness, the whole over-stuffed Politburo sitting so deep in our souls. We could be like two people who inject themselves with truth serum and at long last have to tell it, the truth. I want to be able to say to myself, 'I bled truth with her,' yes, that's what I want. Be a knife for me, and I, I swear, will be a knife for you: sharp but compassionate" (8).

The metaphor of the knife produces a disturbing image; we imagine the one who wants to get in flaying our skin with a sharp knife. Yair captures our paradoxical desire for and fear of exposure when he describes to Miriam the nakedness not of passion, but of "peeled skin"—the kind of nakedness that you can hardly stand "without shock and a quick escape into clothes" (37). He longs for the removal of armor, when the "exertion of hiding and covering and disguising" gives way (38). The daydream continues as Yair imagines an entire street full of people submitting to this urge, running naked in the streets until the "Modesty Squads"—wearing asbestos gloves to avoid touching bodies with bare hands—show up to catch the naked people. And there is that metaphoric use of the knife again: "I always think, a naked person will cut through dressed people like a knife; the clothed will shrink back as if from an infectious disease or an open wound." You can't hate a naked person, Yair writes. You can't fight a naked soldier (38).

What does it take to ask a lover to be your knife, sharp but compassionate? Courage, no doubt—to walk naked, without armor, at great risk of repulsing another with the exposure of your insides. Trust that the lover will use his knife compassionately not to injure but to bleed truth with you, to peel the skin that separates you and overcome strangeness. Mutual desire to get to that place where one can simply say, "tell me where it hurts" (8).

But if the truth is buried beneath skin that is thick with scars and protected with an armor that is impenetrable, and if the repulsion against exposure is irremediable, chances are great that the knife will become a weapon of self-defense.

Yair's growing dependency on Miriam is reminiscent of Simone de Beauvoir's woman in love, who longs to breathe the very air her lover has expelled. He experiences himself as an inessential man and yearns to be fulfilled through the love of a woman. But what limits Yair's love for Miriam is his inability to see her as a separate person; he does not want to *let her be*. He wants to overcome *her* "strangeness," not his own. Through the course of their letters, it becomes clear that despite his desire to be vulnerable to her, he remains unable or unwilling to see himself through her eyes and therefore cannot see that he is slowly stealing from her what she *should not* give. Is this not the very condition for love: to be able to look back at yourself through your lover's eyes, to see the world as she sees it in order to prevent the tyranny of your own ego from subduing hers?

In the end, as Yair's desperation becomes painful for the reader to witness, his metaphoric knife does indeed become a weapon. When Miriam is finally given a voice through the inclusion of her letters and diary entries in the final third of the book, we discover that Yair's desire to be known is the desire for Miriam to be absorbed into his own life—like a blood transfusion, her life coursing through his veins. His love is not for Miriam as a person with her own desires and needs and her own capacity for love and action. On the contrary, by eliminating the foreignness between them, he essentially devours her. Miriam's voice is swallowed up by his own. The knife Yair describes as an instrument of compassion and tenderness becomes an instrument of consumption when he encounters the actual Miriam—Miriam the person who resists his consumption—and she becomes intolerably stuck in his throat, indigestible.

From Miriam's perspective, it is Yair who has told the story (and, indeed, for most of the novel we hear only Yair's voice), and his telling of it has robbed her of her own telling: "Yair, I wanted badly to tell you about yourself, your story was even more important to me than my own. And now I feel I have lost my story" (248). This she writes to herself, no longer in letters that Yair will read. The conversation—the *movement* of love— has ceased with Yair's inability to see himself from an external vantage point. He remains imprisoned in his own narcissistic worldview. Miriam thinks back to the moment when Yair watched her at the reunion without her awareness and reflects on what it is he wants to take from her:

> What I gave him, that thing that spoke to him from deep inside me that, without my knowledge, revived him in this way; the thing between me and myself . . .
>
> I know it exists. It existed before he looked at me, too. It still exists, even if there is no one to look at it now. *It is the good in me*, and it cannot be destroyed. And thanks to that, I cannot be destroyed. If only I could give that to myself as well right now. Just like that. To release it . . . watch it spring out . . .
>
> (249, emphasis added,
> suspension points in original)

This good that cannot be destroyed is Miriam's capacity to be vulnerable to another, to accept the risk that the other might hurt her. It is her ability to live with the exposure of her own nakedness, trusting in her own strength to draw back when necessary.

But Miriam is ambivalent about her intimacy with Yair. She notes in her diary how little they spoke of things "outside the closed circle"—the "bubble"—they inhabited. How long could such an exchange continue without the nourishment of everyday reality, "how much time would have passed until that density would have become suffocation?" she asks and then adds a parenthetical remark: "(Yet now, at this moment, I feel once more that it is in just this kind of density that I could truly start breathing)" (263). The truth is in the parentheses. Acknowledging that she had never before experienced such a mix of pleasure and pain as she had with Yair during their correspondence, Miriam nevertheless admits she would once again welcome him if he could be there for her: "I need for you to flow into me completely, unstintingly. I need it terribly, as one needs air to breathe" (265).

This is not simply masochism, as someone might infer from Miriam's desire for the man who threatened to take what was good in her. It is not the suffocation that gives her pleasure, but the intimacy that comes so close to its edge. Autonomy— the kind that assumes the self as sovereign—can interfere with another's vulnerability. This is apparent in the end and the crisis point of *Be My Knife*. Yair is engaged in a battle of wills with his five-year-old son, Ido, punishing him for his stubbornness by leaving him outside the house until he apologizes for an act of disobedience. Yair goes too far, leaving the unrepentant Ido outside in the cold and rain for hours, hungry and barely dressed. Yair still refuses to relent, insisting to Miriam that he can't let himself show any weakness to Ido. This is the logical conclusion of a battle for autonomy defined by the competition of wills to control the other's freedom. But there must be mercy, and this is what Miriam tries to tell Yair, who persists in his refusal and instead joins Ido in his naked exposure to the elements outside the house. This is where Miriam finds them huddled together, barely conscious, victims of Yair's refusal of risk and, consequently, of love (273–307).

It may be that Miriam's love for Yair and her need for the flow of their intimacy could have withstood his crippling desire. She might have held on to the good in her, preventing him from taking it from her, continuing to love his brokenness. But his abuse of Ido was the limit. This was the act that threatened her capacity for love, the act that threatened mutilation.

Grossman has given us insight into the two dangers noted by Gillian Rose: that we might be either too bounded or too unbounded by the borders between us. We might see ourselves exclusively through the other's eyes or exclusively through our own. There is only one story, then. We can give and give and give until the "good" in us is threatened. And then we reach the limit.

CAN'T OR WON'T

It no longer matters what it was you were berating me for—although I could never forget. What matters is that you aimed for my best thing, *the good in me.* You sat on the bed beside me as I wept in protest against the distorted image you mirrored back to me. You sat with detached calm in that room, barring the door, watching me choke on the words you force-fed me. You argued against the good in me with the conviction of a man of God or with the logical certainty of the most rational of philosophers, as though it were a fact that everyone must know, like the sky is blue. But since you felt this cold rage against my best thing, I knew it was there, large enough to pose a threat to you. The more I shrank under your words, the more you expanded into that room, inflated by your victory.

I felt you tearing out my heart, then all my organs one by one. Perhaps you didn't want to, but we often do what we don't want to do or what we vow we will never do again. In rare moments of clarity, in those fragile moments that arise only under the cover of darkness, we might even own up to these acts of self-sabotage. But mostly we don't. We can't or won't, and we may never know which of these conditions our attitudes and motivates our actions.

In the end, does it matter whether a person can't or won't take responsibility for harming another? We run in mad circles searching for answers to another's destructive behavior, ready to excuse and console, understand and forgive. But the effects are the same—we become the feeding grounds for the insatiable. Every morning we wake up missing small parts of ourselves. We think: I can live with less, you need it more, I have more to give, I will fatten you with love. We think: it isn't your fault, you never had enough love, you don't mean to hurt me, you were hurt, I can handle this. We think this until we no longer know there is any difference between can't and won't, and it dawns on us that we have come to believe that for some it is necessary to destroy in order to survive, even if we are the sacrificial objects. Or maybe it doesn't dawn on us at all because we believe they can't, they truly *can't*, which leads to the unjustifiable conclusion that everything is our fault and that if we just continue to absorb all their negative emotions, we can help them to survive.

What irony, for it was you who slowly lost bits of yourself to disease, whose organs were slowly breaking down, you who did to me exactly what you accused others of doing to you, all the while claiming I was one of them, responsible for all the ills of your life.

THE ANGRYMAN AND THE SWEETMAN

"The wolf who contains, hides or reveals an unexpected sweetness in his violence" is a paradoxical figure, Hélène Cixous writes. "Clearly, the fact that there is sweetness in the wolf makes the sweetness sweeter than the banal sweetness of naturally sweet people. The sweetness of the cruel is a greater sweetness."[7]

I was falling in love with this man who walked before me, talking about his anger toward me after I said something that displeased him. He was a pace or two ahead of me, pulled along by his dog. With the help of his therapist, I was told, he was working on his problem with anger repression. So on this brisk evening walk in November, he happily released his anger into the wind and my trusting heart and felt liberated. I trotted along apologetically behind this Angryman and his eager dog and wondered if his therapist would help me work on my problem with angry men.

My original Angryman was God. I learned from the beginning that love and anger come from the same source, demanding obedience. God was angry enough to throw disobedient children into a pit of fire, where they would burn forever. Although we believed he loved us unconditionally, his anger stuck in our minds as more significant than his capacity to forgive.

Then came my Angryman-father and the occasional Angryman-boyfriends. I learned at a young age how to negotiate tempers. How to soothe, indulge, plead, or remain silent and how to calculate which of these responses was appropriate for the particular occasion. I learned that moods can change on a dime, improve with dessert, and that love can be earned with good behavior. I learned to accommodate the needs of Angrymen to avoid experiencing their anger. I learned to compliment, to stroke egos, to reflect "the figure of man at twice its natural size" in order to preempt his anger.[8] No one told me there was anything wrong with this picture.

The Angryman and the Sweetman inhabit the same body but look quite different. The Angryman has a withering look that shrinks me to the size of a small child, like Alice in Wonderland after eating the wrong cake. His eyes are cold and condescending. He spits words that generally contradict with uncanny exactness the words of the Sweetman. Under the shower of his arrows, beautiful turns to ugly, brilliant to stupid, beloved to wretched, loved to hated.

The Angryman's anger is an effective method of control. This feature distinguishes his kind of anger from another. We get angry at the stupidity of the world's leaders, at those who justify war, poverty, inequality. We get angry when someone wrongs us, when we are not respected, when a stranger is rude, when our children bully their friends or lie to us, when our loved ones ignore our needs. But the Angryman loses his temper because he can't control what we do, think, or say. When we don't follow his orders, he is angry that we have not realized that his plan for us is superior to our own. He is angry when we don't make him feel at all times like the man he believes he is. The Angryman doesn't want his worldview challenged, so he resents our intelligence, our questions, and our criticisms.

Angrymen tell us that if we are not expressing our anger, it means we are simply internalizing our aggression; that anger will manifest itself in one neurosis or another. They can never accept that we don't feel the same anger they do or see that we can live without it. But if and when we do express our anger, they simply bring out the bigger guns to make sure we never do so again.

The Angryman turns into the Sweetman in a flash, purging his negative emotions with stunning speed. He spews the hot lava of his fury until our burned flesh peels off and we feel small and inside-out, and then he stops as suddenly as he started. The air is purged of ash, the sun comes out, he smiles at us with love, and so grateful are we for the appearance of the Sweetman that we forget the Angryman.

But we forget at our peril. If we ever speak this truth to the Angryman, he will punish us without mercy—even kill us if he is angry enough—and we will never again see him as the Sweetman.

ABUSION

I'm tired of being the villain, you said as you busied yourself cutting me with the sharp edge of words, carving your own name into my skin so you could rid yourself of it. A skilled tattoo artist injecting words that slowly congealed into dark lumps.

Look up the word *abuse* in a dictionary, and you find something like this: to use wrongly or improperly (*to abuse one's authority*); improper treatment (*drug abuse*); physical maltreatment; to treat in a harmful, injurious, or offensive way; the act of violating sexually (*rape*); to speak insultingly, harshly, and unjustly to or about someone; to revile or malign.[9] An etymological dictionary tells us that in the early fourteenth century the noun form *abusion* in Old English meant "wicked act or practice, shameful thing, violation of decency." Shortly afterward it became *abuse*, meaning "to insult." By the 1550s, the term was applied to sexual practices such as prostitution, homosexuality, incest: to *misuse* sexually, to ravish.[10]

The idea that abuse is the misuse of something or someone provides an appropriate starting ground for thinking about its meaning. We might even stop at the "use" of another person, for no one should be treated instrumentally as a means toward an end. But this is only a point of departure, for there is a subjective element to abuse—what one person finds intolerable, another might find bearable. How intensely we feel the impact of others' behavior toward us determines how much power we permit them to hurt us. There are obvious misuses of another human being: when one is forced to perform sexual acts or slave labor or when someone is physically injured or killed by a lover. But the members of a couple who hurl epithets in an argument are not necessarily behaving abusively toward each other. Their exchange of insults might be aggression rather than misuse.

If Julia Kristeva is right, "love probably always includes a love for power."[11] At issue here is not merely power, however, but respect for one's person.

An ever-broadening spectrum of behaviors is now called "abusive," subject to cultural interpretation and historical amendment—an expansion that has benefited the moral fabric of human life in obvious ways. It was once acceptable for men to beat their wives or children, and in some places in the world it still is. Although rape is not everywhere considered abuse, we have come a long way in recognizing and punishing this form of violence. But in recent decades we might say the term *abuse* has been applied rather expansively to a range of harms—to "the violation of decency," as the Old English term *abusion* stipulates—as have the labels *victim* and *trauma*. The moral status we have granted to victimhood, combined with the current popularity of confession, encourages us to believe we all are victims of something or someone and must tell the story to recover from our traumas.[12] Severe abuse—such as sexual or physical violation—renders trivial the nebulous dictionary definitions of abuse as treating someone in an "offensive" way or speaking "harshly" to another. Our increasing intolerance of bullying and insulting has no doubt had beneficial outcomes. But if too many actions are lumped together under the term *abuse*, it loses its meaning. Definitions are necessary because we need to make judgments against actions that harm others, but we need to wield them skeptically, aware of the dangers of simplistic dichotomies. The risk of labeling is that we might forget there are degrees of harm and degrees of responsibility for it—and an ever-present gray zone.

How can we judge harm or misuse given these complexities? Some consider consent to be the only criterion, but this is not as simple as it sounds. Consider the number of times we hear about a woman who refuses to press charges against an abusive partner or leave him. Consent is subject to context, influence, conscious and unconscious proclivities; it implies that we make decisions and engage in behavior as absolutely free beings. Judgments about abuse have to be context specific; subjective and objective factors as well as levels of power and levels of suffering must be taken into account. Judging an act as right or wrong is only a beginning—it is the effects of an act that beg deliberation.

I am wary of this work of classifying or labeling harmful human behavior for generalized purposes and so use the term *abuse* with more than a little reluctance. But there is relief in the victim who finally has a name for his or her experience. The term *abuse* conjures up the worst scenarios: battered women, tortured

men, sexually violated or beaten children. As a result, the use of
the term affirms for victims of maltreatment that something very
wrong has occurred to them. The importance of this affirmation
should not be underestimated. There is relief in knowing that
what has happened to you has not happened *only* to you, that it
has a wider social context, meaning that others might understand
it and feel what you feel. Naming abuse is like diagnosing the
disease you suffer from: symptoms are not random but form a
pattern and have been documented by others. Support is more
easily solicited; one may find communities of other sufferers with
whom to share information about illness and personal struggles.
Most important is the relief from self-blame. Naming is part of
assigning responsibility. Imagine the relief of the child who never
knows what to call this recurring, secret violation that induces
shame and self-recrimination but who suddenly finds out it has a
name—it is a wrongful act called "sexual abuse." In the naming is
confirmation that he is indeed suffering and not as a result of his
own actions. But more than this, he discovers that he is not alone
against his tormentor; others will assure him that what has been
done to him is wrong and will stand with him against the wrong-
doer. In this respect, the risk of overdetermining a term such as
abuse seems worth taking.

The psychological effects of physical abuse or of the kind of
misuse that does not penetrate the borders of the body are often
invisible and thus harder to classify. But at the core of the experience of abuse, physical or psychological, is the absence of respect.

Whether one is actually gagged and bound to a chair or belit-
tled into silence; whether one is slapped for disobeying or told
one will never amount to anything; whether one is beaten until
one bleeds or subjected to a daily barrage of insults—at issue is
essentially respect for another's freedom to be. *Let me be*, cries the

victim of abuse, exhausted from being held down. I do not mean freedom in the sense of license to do whatever one wants, regardless of what others want, but freedom as agency.

In other words, although we are always in relation to others, we are also individual selves and must determine the course of our lives as best we can within the limitations of an unpredictable world and our own mortality. Abuse—to varying degrees—is constituted by the negation of another's freedom to be. This negation is the opposite of "volo ut sis"—the inexplicable affirmation of another person that is the manifestation of love. The misuse of another is a violation of the boundaries signified by skin and individual agency and responsibility; abuse occurs in the absence of respect for the separateness of another individual. It is fundamentally about control.

A MISNOMER

Your survival appeared to depend on projecting everything despicable onto me, words your weapon of choice. The border between the mind and the body is a porous one, rendering *"At least he didn't hit you"* a misnomer. Pain and suffering travel quickly between psyche and body; attacks targeting one may be felt on the other—words felt like small knives, insults like kicks to the teeth—because words in this case are not isolated events. They form part of a larger strategy designed to make us feel small and unworthy for the purposes of control and manipulation, strategized after careful calculation of our vulnerabilities.

If I could be made to feel the anguish of your soul, you would feel it a little less. Your survival depended on pushing me to the very edge of disaster and expecting me to return, every time—my return the proof of the unconditional love you craved. An eternal repetition of what Freud called the "fort-da" game. And my survival depended on surrendering to your worldview.

Physical abuse is the easiest to define; it is tangible and usually visible. Its effects are immediate and evident and therefore all the more alarming. A bruised face or broken limb might be called an accident, but at least no one can deny that something happened. Psychological abuse is defined as causing some form of trauma to a victim by acts, threats of acts, or coercive tactics. The Centers for Disease Control include in their definition such behaviors as humiliation, control, withholding information, annoyance when the victim disagrees, and deliberately making someone feel diminished, but these behaviors are only a few arbitrary examples. Some might think them trivial, and as isolated events they might be. But they become relentless, a private version of low-intensity warfare or the kind of torture that is declared within the law and therefore not really torture, designed to wear us down until we are weary and defenseless.

Those who intentionally or unintentionally cause another's suffering may very well be suffering themselves, granting them a perfect alibi. Their bullying or cruelty is not labeled as such by those who love them and become the targets of their abuse, thanks to clever manipulation. But the manipulation and the cruelty that result are also invisible to others. There is no better way to hide abusive behavior than to discredit the victim, to isolate her from close friends who might provide a more accurate picture of the relationship dynamics, and to make her doubt her own judgment. All of this is far easier when bullies are or were victims themselves. When the perpetrators' own suffering is evident, the pain of their victims is often ignored by others. For the *victims of victims*, the refusal to acknowledge their pain can be as debilitating as the abuse. There is little hope that the truth will matter to anyone if the victim who victimizes is empowered by the moral authority of his or her own suffering.

This dynamic is largely ignored in current discussions of bullying or abuse, as though we expect the genuine bully to be without a complicated past, to be *purely* a perpetrator, without her own experiences of victimhood, so that we will have no qualms calling her to account for her actions. We resist acknowledging the ambiguities of abuse because we cannot accept that a person who harms another might be both lovable and loving. We like to think that evil has one face and that we will always recognize it. The reality is often quite different. In our search for the abusive person who matches the pure villain of our imaginations, we fail to see the one standing before us. And so we remain blind to the complexity both of the person who abuses a loved one and of the dynamic between them.

Such blindness is the desired outcome of the one who manipulates—the person whose survival appears to depend on controlling another, who works hard to cover his tracks. We underestimate the intelligence and skill this requires, for the one who survives by harming others must keep the manipulation a great secret—not only from others, but from himself and from the person he manipulates. What better way than to ensure that his victim believes everything is her fault? It is hard work, for he has to persuade everyone outside of his sphere of abuse that he is sweet and charming. It will help him later when he must persuade the world that he himself is the victim of abuse, not this person who has come forward to accuse him. He must calculate, lay his traps early, anticipate errors, come up with contingency plans, stay vigilant against the truth at all costs by creating a public persona that will endear and protect him.

And those of us who find ourselves manipulated? A world of deception and misery is contained within the awkward term *manipulatable*. Think of the suffering caused by the greatest political ideologies we know—fascism or Nazism—and the thousands who denied their own responsibility by throwing up their hands and saying, "We were merely following orders!" Think of the religious cults whose fanatic leaders hold such power over their followers that if instructed to kill themselves, they comply, like sheep led to the slaughter. Consider the propaganda that incites one politicized group to label another *un*human to justify killing them—and in no time the machetes are brought out.

The more vulnerable and trusting we are, the easier we are to manipulate. The child in a church pew, told she will burn in the fires of hell for her wrongdoing, might be terrified enough to conform, to believe, to banish all doubt. Break her down to expose her naked fears and longings, and she becomes malleable, dependent on the one who seeks control—for approval, love, or simply the necessity of her existence—and therefore *useful* to the manipulator. When her desire is reduced to pleasing God, discovering his will, living solely for him, she could be asked to do just about anything in God's name. Including satisfying the sexual desires of the one who calls himself a man of God, whom she was taught to trust.

Military training operates on this principle. Break the recruits down, erase their individual identities, beat them up verbally until they are nothing without the approval of their superiors, until all they long for is a word of praise for an act of courage, physical prowess, heroism. Then they go willingly into the hell of combat and do the unspeakable things required of them without question. A soldier who questions, like the religious person who doubts his faith, is no longer useful.

Those who have experienced a loved one's controlling behavior will recognize themselves here, too. The process of manipulation might be long and slow, but it works like the most efficient military training. There is the seductive promise of love, mutual desire, and gratification—any self-help book will tell you about the ecstatic beginnings of some of the most manipulative and abusive relationships—before the gradual process of destroying the will, siphoning out the soul, until there is only a shell of a person left. A *useful* shell, dependent on the love and approval of the person who seduced her so expertly, who drew her in with the most exquisite displays of vulnerability and tenderness, for whom she will now do almost anything. And so we have another kind of hell.

None of us likes to admit how vulnerable we are to manipulation—some of us much more so than others. There is a social stigma against being sucked in, gullible, emotionally vulnerable, not intelligent or strong enough to know when someone is taking us for a ride. But some people are just very good at manipulating, assuming such a clever disguise for their need to control that almost everyone is fooled. The victim of such a person might be lonely, indeed. We, too, are trying to survive.

THE PARADOX OF RISK

A surprising blind spot: our liberal doctrines of happy love assume that because abuse is the antithesis of love, the two can never coexist in the private world of the couple. But love does not inoculate us against violence. If we assume those who love us would never hurt us, we may not see—or may refuse to see—when we are wronged by our lovers, negated at the most naked level.

This is the human condition—we love, but we also hate; we are kind and compassionate but also aggressive and mean. In an intimate world of two, when there is so much love that there is also the fear of losing it, when there is enough vulnerable exposure to fill a house with white light, we would have to work very hard to remain blind to our lovers' darker sides. Life and love in close proximity to another require a constant recognition of another person's beauty and flaws, strengths and weaknesses. We must hold these contradictory qualities together without dividing our loved ones into good and bad selves. It becomes an impossible effort when the lover himself lives a doubled existence and projects all that is bad onto his beloved to be free of it himself. She becomes unable to hold herself together. This is her undoing.

In the face of love, we disarm ourselves, which is what Hélène Cixous explains constitutes our greatest risk. We have a relationship of absolute vulnerability with those we love because we believe the person who loves us will not harm us at the same time that we think this person is the only one who can do all the harm in the world to us. Experience bears this out—our dearest love might abandon us, leave us by dying, or even kill us. And so "in love we know we are at the greatest risk and at the least great risk, *at the same time.*"[13] We have here the great paradox of love, for the vulnerability that leads to this risk is our best thing. It should not surprise us that we might be more likely to harm those we love most dearly than complete strangers. In part, this is because we care more about what our lovers think of us, and this means we lend them the power to hurt us. Vulnerability is the condition of love, yes, but it is also the condition of abuse.

Knowing we are loved, we accept behavior or actions from our lovers that we would never accept from anyone else. We may schizophrenically hold the love and the pain together until we are no longer able to pry them apart. We might never even know they do not belong together. Child abuse by a parent or close relative provides our best example here. Imagine the confusion of the toxic mix—affection and love might alternate with humiliation and insult, or beating and rape. The child absorbs the love and the pain together, the sweet always poisoned by the bitter.

We seem unable to accept this contradiction, so we reduce the dynamic of the relationship to something easier to diagnose: masochism, for example, the "battered woman syndrome" writ large, extended to any case in which we love someone who causes us pain. Masochism means we experience pleasure in the pain. But those who are abusive might also be capable of great love and affection. We might experience them as split beings—the hostile and the sweet, the violent and the tender. The pleasure is in the sweet and the tender, but to procure it we must endure the violence.

What if the love overwhelms personal suffering, becomes larger and more powerful? It may be that what gives us pleasure in this case—what we love and long for—is the end of the torment of those who torment others, including us. We might be willing to sacrifice something—too much—to relieve this torment. But here we stand on a precipice, risking our own destruction through the kind of compassion that allows the abuse to continue. One of the hardest tasks for many people is to focus on the truth— the facts and the effects of the abuse—rather than on the reasons they might use to justify it. Compassion or neutrality might give rise to more victims or at least do nothing to prevent them. Blinded by our own compassion and benevolence, we might not notice the skill of the manipulator, coaxing this compassion from us. Because that is precisely what he needs to go on justifying his own behavior to himself and everyone else. We have unwittingly become his accomplices in the marvelous performance of the victimizer who plays the victim.

Our friends might be more clear-visioned, as mine were, who told me as often as I needed to hear it: "You have the right to leave. No one should bar the door."

THE HOUSE OF TRAGEDY

The truth is always in the house. Silent walls bear witness to it, absorb the sharp words and broken cups without complaint. Coffee stains in the corner where the rag missed, the day it was too much for one person to handle. Too much need pulling this way and that. Too much need thwarted and then disguised, fused into knives, aimed and flung with precision. Too much fear.

The face of a house is stolid, betraying little of the struggles within. From the sidewalk, we see white slats cross a windowpane, dark curtains, the yellow of lights beyond. A cat might languish, indifferent, on the sill. The rhythm and tenor of life only a vague hint through this window—motion and stillness, desire and disappointment, love and anguish expand and contract with every breath inside those walls. And sometimes collapse.

If only the walls divulged their dark secrets. If only the mute figures on the mantel chose to speak or the cat renounced his obstinate vow of silence. No edifice of lies would survive their judgment.

In my dreams, the house I left spills its cache of secrets, images without definition or punctuation, this scene blending into that one, no temporal truth to order them: *There you slept with your head on my lap or read amusing lines to me at the table we laughed over our books and kissed while leaning against the kitchen counter there you are at the door to greet me your embrace lifting me off the ground and later I am weightless floating somewhere between our love and our desire there is the spindle I broke when I threw my boot at you in fury the overturned wheelchair that day when tensions were high and there the refuge of the backyard where I wept with the trees as my witnesses and the commiseration of squirrels where I spent so many hours trying to understand your torment adjusting always adjusting my responses when you took my keys so I would not leave because you loathed your dependency and spurned my care and there in the parking lot of Shoppers I listened to Renée Fleming soar through the notes of Ave Maria with wings I wanted for myself bewildered as I was by the twists and turns in the heart's Antarctic[14] and the terrors of your soul there on the back porch I left my plants to die when I fled and could not fit them in the car there the ivy climbed and choked despite all my attempts to cut it back pull it out by its herculean roots a metaphor for our life in the house of our tragedy and always always the echo of your words alternately bursting with love or cruelty like a dramatic accompaniment to memory.*

THE LINE

How do we know when we have crossed over that line from compromise and negotiation for the sake of love to giving what should never be taken, what should never be asked of us to give?

I did not know until that morning when my friend asked me, "How often could you tolerate this behavior from him?" And I answered without hesitating: once a week. From the look he gave me, I understood it as a trick question. I could no longer deny that I was on the wrong side of the line, so persuaded of the new normal of my life that tolerating the intolerable once a week seemed an acceptable compromise for the sake of love, that this was simply life, what anyone would do to keep the peace. I had no lexicon for this dynamic, nothing to help me see with any clarity what was happening to me. Nothing of what I knew as an educated, intelligent person, strong of character for the most part, more practiced in self-reflection than the average person, made this transparent. There are reasons for this blind spot that we often ignore: we do not sign on to a relationship that we know is one day going to find us throwing mugs of coffee out of anguish, defeated by insults, and locked out of our homes in our slippers. We fall in love with a complicated, troubled person who is both lovable and wounded, equally capable of affection and fury, who unravels slowly, only after we have proved ourselves trusting, eager to please, and easy to manipulate.

When we do not understand what is happening to us, we must ask our friends, those we trust, to observe us from a perspective outside the circus ring of our unconscious entanglements. Those who want to control their lovers know this well, which is why they work so diligently to isolate them from friends and from the world in general. There are physical methods of imprisonment and then there are psychological methods of control: make sure the victim no longer trusts herself, keep her on edge, second-guessing herself, doubting her friends until she comes to believe that there is only one objective reality and that it belongs to the person who both loves and torments her.

I have sought to understand psychological abuse without yielding to the temptation of platitudes. But we have acquired an enormous vocabulary on abuse that sometimes serves us well. In the thick of it, we need to know, quickly, that what is happening to us is not an isolated experience. We need to call a spade a spade. This is emergency thinking. There is time later for insight into the contradictions and nuances of the experience. Our own denial is part of the problem—it keeps us bobbing up and down in the currents of excuses, apologies, and endless unfulfilled promises.

I have never stopped asking why I loved someone who was destructive. I have never stopped trying to understand. In this process, we find ourselves engaged in the work of justification: ashamed to admit to being susceptible to manipulation; guilt-ridden when we reflect back on what we feel were weak responses when strength was called for; exposed when we turn ourselves inside out and let others observe the turmoil there.

Barry Lopez, a victim of nearly four years of sexual abuse as a boy, writes that when he began therapy, he speculated that "the real horror of those years" would be the actual details of the abuse—the choking, the bleeding, the silencing—but he discovered it was more elusive. "The enduring horror was that I had learned to accommodate brutalization," Lopez explains; "caught up in someone else's psychosis, overmatched at every turn, I had concentrated on only one thing: survival. To survive I needed to placate."[15] This is the particular burden of the victim of abuse, wondering how this happened to him in particular, why he did not stop it or expose the abuser, if it were even in his power to do so—questions that might look different years later.

It is well known that victims of sexual abuse and assault often blame themselves. It was suggested to me once that the reason for this self-blame might be that they are so terrified by random events, they prefer causal explanations, even those that put the onus on the victims. In this way, they impose some control over the unpredictable nature of life. If they had not been walking on that street or so intent on pleasing, if they had had more self-esteem or confidence, then this terrible thing would never have happened. This reassures them, for in the future they believe they will be smarter, stronger, and capable of preventing similar terrible things from happening.

But when we love the person who harms us, when we are "overmatched at every turn," we should not blame ourselves for trying to survive. We did not choose for it to happen the way it did.

Surprisingly, it might be harder to forgive ourselves than to forgive the person who harmed us.

A BAD CALCULATION

You called me "Israel" that day and slammed the door. A small country, but the irony was vast. As if I were equipped with the arsenal of the most powerful military in the world. As if I were the victim immunized by the moral authority of my crippled psyche and diseased body. As if I could justify brutality with the fact of my history of suffering. But that is how it looked from where you stood. You said you were compelled to pull out the bigger guns when you felt attacked, but when you told me that, I did not yet know that you perpetually felt attacked.

Reading Freud on the unconscious leaves me marveling that any of us manages to develop and survive intimacy with another human being. In the vast and unknowable territory below the surface of our conscious selves lurk the ghosts of our pasts—they dog us in our dreams or unguarded moments. The unconscious is a swampy region, full of repressed emotions, desires, and impulses. It holds far too much that is mysterious and inaccessible for us to classify human behavior into precise categories. Even our conscious selves can confuse us.

Above the surface, we tell soothing stories to distract ourselves from what lingers below. Anything to resist looking: repression, projection, lies, jokes, blame. We have an arsenal of weapons at our disposal to defend ourselves from what we might suspect is there but really do not want to see. This is what makes any love relationship maddeningly complicated, but some far more than others. We let our lovers into those vulnerable places where they might glimpse a ghost or two without alarm. We may not need an elaborate defense system if we are both willing to allow someone in and able to look long and hard ourselves. But the more turmoil there is below, the harder we have to work to keep the lid on. A more sophisticated defense system might be required to warn anyone who tries to lift that lid. But then we face the risk of self-destruction—those weapons have a way of backfiring. Fear and paranoia, as Othello discovered, may conspire to bring about the very outcome most dreaded. The lover unwittingly kills his own love, a slow, painful strangulation of a love no longer remembered as anything but the deception and rejection that were feared.

No one describes this dynamic better than Israeli author David Grossman, although his context is not two individual psyches in conflict but two peoples. "To live in a disaster zone means to be clenched, both physically and emotionally," he explains in *Writing in the Dark*, "the muscles of the body and the soul are alert and tensed, ready for fight or flight." But when a state tries to secure itself from all risk, as Israel has done, a "cruel reversal" takes place, a point at which it no longer matters whether or when the feared danger will actually occur because the fear of it has already created the danger within. The constant fear of humiliation leads to a routine saturated with it. Life is conducted "within the fear of fear," and anxiety slowly distorts the nature of the individual as well as society, robbing everyone of happiness and purpose.[16]

No one can adapt to such conditions without paying a high price, Grossman warns, in fact the highest price: "the price of living itself, the price of sensitivity, of humanity, of curiosity, and of liberty of thought. The fear of and aversion to facing others fully and soberly: not only the enemy, but *any others*." Soon enough everyone becomes an enemy, and under the cloak of so much protection we are threatened by suffocation.[17]

Grossman concludes: "I fear that after decades of spending most of our energies, our thoughts and attention and inventiveness, our blood and our life and our financial means, on protecting our external borders, fortifying and safeguarding them more and more—after all this, we may be very close to becoming like a suit of armor that no longer contains a knight, no longer contains a *human*."[18] This is what happens to those who can no longer live with their own vulnerability. Love can fail to disable their defense systems. The lover may find herself the very intruder against whom the guns are aimed for the sake of survival.

Destructive and self-destructive behaviors attest to the power of the unconscious. We might claim that such behaviors are the fault of genetic or environmental inheritance. We might excuse all destructive acts on the basis of prior victimhood—insisting the perpetrator was once a victim and therefore not culpable for her actions. This is tempting—we do not like to think that someone wants to harm another or enjoys it. It is easier to believe she cannot help it because she is a victim of circumstances beyond her control. Nor do we want to accept that someone who harms others cannot be reformed.

Cixous asks: "What is it that makes human beings find satisfaction in destruction?" Everyone ultimately chooses life, she responds. Some choose their own survival even if it means killing others—destruction is their means of living, a "bad calculation."

And some choose to save others in order to survive. Two means of survival: the origin of all conflicts.[19] But if we accept that someone's survival requires the harm or even death of another, we accept both murder and suicide.

For Grossman, the antidote to this paradox of survival by self-destruction is to understand or know the "enemy" from within him. This means not to love one's enemy but to "read reality through the enemy's eyes." As in any individual relationship, this encounter entails relinquishing "our sophisticated defense mechanisms" and exposing ourselves to the feelings of others, even of our enemies.[20] And so we return, once again, to the condition for loving—to be vulnerable enough to look at ourselves through another's eyes.

SWEET REVENGE

If only relationships began at their end, for this is when we disclose ourselves most fully, when we discover what means of survival an ego will employ to protect itself from pain.

Vengeance is your inoculation. You are riding high on the blood you drew from my exposed veins, the triumph of revenge preventing you from drowning. If you can persuade the world that I am despicable, you can be good, worthy, and lovable, freed from your persistent self-loathing.

I struggle with the negation of being cast off, my idiosyncrasies no longer endearing, my desirability diminished. The energy directed toward me is withdrawn, leaving in its wake abandonment and betrayal. I have to fight for dignity, fortifying myself with the affirmation of those who know and love me, discounting your opinion, held so dear. Once I was the best thing that ever happened to you; now I am worthless. I stand destitute before this wall of hatred, small and negated, all of my best things destroyed, and my worst things magnified into gross caricatures. The intimate world we cultivated is now blown open and bits of my life lie scattered and exposed to the world's gaze, like the things you refused to return—private words I wrote to myself, material things that suddenly acquired the significance of pieces of me left behind. The image of my self reflected in your adoring gaze is cut up and rearranged without sense or coherence. More than the loss of love, I experience the loss of meaning, value, home, and I wonder who I am now, who I will become without you.

To be hated ranks among the most unpleasant of human experiences. Feelings of worth, of the value of our place in the world, are dependent on those we live among, in particular those closest to us. We want what is best in us to be reflected by those we love, and when our best is mirrored back to us, we flourish. We want to please our friends and lovers; we want to be loved. So we cultivate those qualities in our characters that draw others to us. Of course, we also want to be loved despite our faults, and we hope naïvely that we will be loved by someone who fails to notice we have any faults or tolerates them when they make their appearance.

There is no defense against someone we have welcomed freely—through the front door, as it were—who has occupied all our private rooms, witnessed the dirt in the corners, the mess in the kitchen, and eagerly created a world and a history with us despite this exposure. When the lover makes us into the enemy, there is nowhere to hide. We are in the home that is our private life, one we both know intimately. It is not a matter of bolting the doors and windows. He is already in the house, wrecking havoc with our insides.

Reasonable explanations are sought for rejection—a tidy narrative and justifications. Unable to put love and hate together, we decide that love was not there to begin with. In our anguish, we accuse, "You never loved me. You could not have loved me if you no longer do." It must have been a mirage, a fantasy. If the person we loved finds another to love, it feels like deception, betrayal. That we are dispensable when we believed ourselves to be indispensable not only changes our present view of the predicament but also revises history as well. Suddenly it was not me who was loved in my absolute singularity. To be replaced means that the words reserved for us only—*you are the love of my life*—are rendered meaningless, for they have become universal rather than particular. We are reduced to the foil for the desirability of the new lover, the standard against which she will be measured and pronounced beautiful to our ugly, adorable to our despised.

It might be that hatred is only as fierce as the love it replaces. The anger, the vindictiveness, even the hatred may not mean that love died or was never there to begin with. On the contrary, it might mean that love was so profound it was painful.

SAVING

It was the prospect of your death that kept me on edge at every moment. You told me once that you nearly died of sepsis; this word hung over our days. In the emergency waiting room, you asked for water, fever clouding your eyes, saturating your skin with sweat. But I had no coins for the dispenser, and the foam cups were stacked beyond the glass in the nurses' station. A thick glass window and a queue of need stood between me and the water that would save your life—this was my panic-induced impression. In such moments, it is our own crisis that matters, nothing and no one else can stand in the way of our sole mission: to save the one we love. How easily we can understand sacrifice—forgetting ourselves in the fierce drive of our will to alleviate suffering.

Miriam Toews describes the ferocity of this will to save in *All My Puny Sorrows*, a work of fiction that is close to the life of its author, who lost both a sister and a father to suicide.[21] Yoli must live with the desperate anxiety of the person who wants to save a loved one bent on self-destruction—her sister, Elfrieda, a talented pianist battling depression who has tried several times to take her own life. Elfrieda begs Yoli to accompany her to Switzerland not only to assist in her suicide but to provide the solace of her presence. Yoli's emotional struggle is a wrenching read, but what is most extraordinary in this story is the unfolding of her awareness that love is not always enough, that there are limits to what one can do for another in love.

It seems a simple claim to make, a self-evident point, that there are two persons involved in any relationship, separated by a border, however flimsy. But it is hardly simple when the desire of one of those persons is to eliminate one of the other's most cherished things. We see Toews grappling with the question of selfishness in love and with this terrible boundary between two people who love each other that forces one to give in to the other's desires even at the cost of life. But we can never be responsible for another's life. To acknowledge our limits might always feel like selfishness and failure. Even if we know that throwing ourselves into deep waters to save a drowning person is a useless sacrifice.

We can fight hard, but we can also acknowledge defeat and stop fighting, Yoli writes in a letter to her dead sister at the end of the novel. "The brain is built to forget things as we continue to live," Yoli's mother has told her, and "memories are meant to fade and disintegrate." The skin sags, and sharp edges—like the pain of letting go of grief—become blunt.[22]

Your fevered delirium, my frantic search for water, the impenetrable barrier between me and what would keep you with me.
How symbolic of our story of love. My impotent gestures on the
wrong side of a thick glass window, through which I could only
glimpse your salvation.

LEAVING

I left you. These words accuse. The one who leaves bears the brunt
of social judgment. As though one could leave one's beloved only
out of selfishness, on impulse, without thinking. But I did feel
selfish. Leaving was the most selfish thing I had ever done. I said
to my mother, "It is cruel to leave," and she replied, "It is cruel to
stay." And there is the limit of love. We can live only our own lives
and love from within the limitations of life. If love requires more
of us, if our love for another demands that we sacrifice what has
allowed us to love, we must save ourselves, pull back from that
precipice before it is too late.

The stigma of leaving overshadows the fact that leaving is
the only right thing to do when the fear of staying has finally
overpowered the fear of leaving. When love dies a natural death,
leaving might be liberating rather than painful. But when there
are other reasons to leave, it might be the hardest thing one has
to do. Very few who stay recognize the courage of those who
leave, insisting instead on the failures of lovers who part ways: to
love *properly*, to commit, and to accept the inevitable transition
from the heady days of erotic beginnings to the ordinary days of
domestic proximity. If longevity is our only standard of measure,
those who choose life over commitment or duty will be objects of
resentment. If loving freely is the basis on which we judge a love,

there is no such thing as failure, and the one who leaves has perhaps chosen honesty and truth over formulas, traded the fear of a living death for the risk of the unknown. I speak not of the restless longing to wander when the fiery days of desire have cooled but of the deep inner discord of not living truthfully with oneself.

There is no way to philosophize the pain out of leaving. Dare I write of that one day when finality impressed itself on every passing moment? Can I describe without the inevitable clichés the dread in my bones as I prepared to swallow the bitter pill: *this is what must be done*? Impossible to move beyond the trite, beyond the sudden shyness of words. In print, these words look as if they come from someone else, bearing little relation to what I felt as I waited for you to leave the house, nearly immobilized by fear at the door. The adrenalin that rushed in to rescue me as I gathered up the pieces of me scattered in those rooms and threw everything in boxes or garbage bags. Or my gratitude for the compassion of the men who arrived to help me, patting me on the shoulders as if I were their little sister in crisis, these strangers who entered my life for a few hours and yet became an integral part of my most wrenching memories.

And the layers of memory keep peeling back, one by one, until I have returned to that highway in a car stuffed with file folders poking through plastic bags, books and plants and framed works of art wedged in the crevices left by boxes of winter coats and office supplies. That highway of my retreat, dangerously blurred by weeping, my body heaving in disbelief because love did not win this time. Because my love was not enough to overcome the sepsis of your unconscious. Because I lost you. Because now I faced gathering up the pieces of me and arranging them in a different order.

PART IV

LOSS

THE ORIGINAL LOSS

OSS is a strange gift, a catalog of all that we have treasured. Without loss, we have had nothing. Without grief, we have never loved.

The first loss, the template of all losses to come, belongs to the infant.

The undifferentiated fetus has no self. It is loved by blood and muscle wall, soothed by muted voices and the steady beat of a woman's heart; the fetus is coddled, nourished. After birth, it finds itself on the outside of the mother's body, physically separate but still undifferentiated, self-less. The infant suffers when detached from the breast and flesh of the mother, limbs flailing anxiously in open air. From the beginning, the trauma of this first separation dogs us; this is the loss of home and absolute security. We bind and we separate throughout our lives, until our final, irrevocable separation in death.

It is the presence or absence of first love that determines how well we survive the ensuing flux.

There is another loss in this event, different from that of the infant. Our most pronounced parental delight occurs when the infant returns our smiles. We encounter each other's faces and light up in recognition and adoration. The infant who reaches for us, dimpled arms encircling our necks, gives us a reason to live. We are paragons of protection. The absolute vulnerability and dependence of babies arouse all that is best in us. Only sometimes do they arouse all that is worst.

That we must separate becomes obvious, and it is a long and painful process. In a mother's love, we possibly find the greatest association between love and loss that we can ever experience. Only loss through death is worse. This is not the same as the original loss the infant experiences, not the loss of home and protection, but the loss of *being* the home and protector. And this means the loss of control—or at least of the perception of control that we had while the fetus was still growing within us—over the fates that might harm our children.

I sit across the table from this young man who was born of me. As soon as I write this line, a world of meaning bursts out of its seams—a world of contradictions. I am absorbed by what he is telling me in the present moment but am also remembering those eyes in a child's face—the same intensity, force of concentration, the same hunger for beauty. His hands, too, the way they gesture, hold a history known better to me than my own.

It seems I have known him since long before his birth, as though there never was a time without him—or only a shadow of one. Yet the years from infant to adult collapse into a moment, memorialized in photographs, crayoned drawings and clay sculptures; a moment teeming with hundreds of images and sensations, fragments dislodged from their timeline. His first of everything: solid food, steps, words, friends, sorrow, suffering, love. My first of a mother's love: fierce and unbending, so full with its other that it is hard to know where one ends and the other begins, terrified of the suffering or loss of he who was born of me.

I have always been losing him in one sense, gaining him in another.

There is no love like this. No love like the one that must, of necessity, grow up with loss—more and more of it as the years wear on—in precisely the same measure as gain. What has left my body and then, slowly, the orbit of my care becomes an individual who is entirely not me. He becomes the person who sits across this table speaking to me as though I were someone else, some wholly separate person. Of course, I *am* someone else and always have been. Yet this fact comes to me as something of a revelation, here, today, at this table. Surely there is no greater joy than to witness this becoming of a person, no matter how painful the slow separation.

If only we always knew this moment of truth. If only we could project ourselves into the future, to this table across which we will talk, knowing this separateness, knowing that an adult lies in wait inside the child. If only we chose to speak to the future selves of our children during those years of innocence when they know not what we do, when we think we do not have to explain ourselves. Then we might pause long enough to ask: What will this future adult say to us? Will there be accusation or forgiveness? Will he know how dearly he was loved?

This is the first loss of many that teaches us how to love *and* separate, how to love *and* relinquish the control we want in order to prevent suffering. If we succeed in managing this difficult dance, we will have learned the secret of "volo ut sis"— of affirming the being of the other beyond any explanation, which is love.

SLOW HEART

The stubborn heart is slow—slow to acknowledge pain beyond one's limits, slow to close against it, slow to forget it.

We use the term *masochism*—defined as the enjoyment of pain—too loosely and misdiagnose the one who persists in loving *in spite of* pain. Such love might be stubborn rather than masochistic. Blind to the writing on the wall, the slow heart refuses to let go when letting go is the only way for both lovers to survive. When the love is already dying, the slow heart beats its steady refusal, believing love can conquer all obstacles, even its own death. Eyes are put out, ears boxed, limbs broken, but the blood of a slow heart roars on.[1] That heart must be bludgeoned into stillness with the brute fact that love is not a cure for every disease. Love can be rejected like an incompatible transplant organ.

And after the rejection of our love, those of us with slow hearts live in a time lag. While we drag our bodies into the present, our senses remain in yesterday's stimuli—breathing in the scent of skin still familiar, our mind's eye lingering over features now memorialized. Asking with Héloise's anguished disbelief in a letter to Abelard, Shall I never see you again? Shall I never embrace you again?

For a long time, we refuse all thought of loving another. We are not yet detached; any new love would constitute an act of betrayal. When we finally entertain possibilities, they disappoint us, only reminding us of what we have lost, only reigniting our desire for the taste of our old love. Familiarity breeds desire as much as it breeds contempt. We have learned the lay of the land with a lover, navigated through storms, languished in gardens we cultivated, which took time, patience, and negotiation. We greet the creation of new worlds with trepidation, wondering how we might trust anew, how we might be courageous enough to be vulnerable once again.

How many nights after I fled did I hear you call my name, your face close to mine with cyclopean love, as you said to me once, one eye buried in your pillow? How many days did I see you walking toward me, love spread across your face? The body's capacity for remembering astounds us. The exquisite softness of mouth on mouth, the taste of salt on skin, the erotic lullaby of a voice—curse or bless the visceral detail of memory—this kiss on an otherwise sad day, those words you sang, that look of desire you gave me. These images play endlessly in the aftermath of love and too slowly lose their power to keep us in the past. But time carries us farther and farther from the event of a love; our memories become less palpable, reduced to a few of the most potent images.

Slow heart.

IRON AIR

The slow heart moves as though through iron air,[2] denying what has come to pass, pulling back on time so hard we think it will reverse, imagining a different history until everything seems more possible than what actually happened. It was all a mistake and will be corrected in due course. I kept this hope while fearing it, removing myself to a foreign city to separate from who I had become and to resist her hold on me, going through the motions of work and routine in the bubble that living alone among foreigners permits. My own voice restricted to ordering coffee or deli items in a foreign language, to please or thank you or excuse me, and to hours and hours of conversing on paper with my now former self. Trying to comprehend the incomprehensible, indulging in guilt and self-recrimination because it was easier to exonerate him than me, easier to accept my responsibility than his, easier to feel compassion for him than for me.

If only hindsight were foresight. If only we could experience in the present the hindsight of our future selves looking back over the years, confident in their understanding of events passed. If only we could have the wisdom that comes through experience before we plunge into the thickness of the now. This might save us, we think, from making the worst of our decisions. Instead we wonder, like the poet Jane Hirshfield who looks back with surprise that life was not as she expected and asks of her future self: "Will she look at me with hatred or with compassion, / I whose choices made her what she will be?"[3]

This is the very defining moment of self-reflection—when we exercise our unique capacity to step out of ourselves just long enough to look at who we are and what we are doing as though considering another person. What better way to deliberate over what we need to do, than to imagine how our decisions and actions in this moment will help define who we are tomorrow? I have a responsibility to that future self—to ensure she will look back on me with compassion, with gratitude for what I decide today.

There is an art to self-reflection, one we must cultivate until it becomes habit and then protect at all cost. It begins with seeing ourselves from another's point of view, whether that other is our future self, our trusted friends in the present, or our own mind's eye. We must try to separate from ourselves—reflect on our perspectives and behavior from the vantage point of another place or time to understand and assess what we are thinking and doing. This is what we do when we ask advice from friends or have intimate conversations about something that has happened to us; we surround ourselves with trusted voices, urging, warning, comforting, or deliberating with us. It is also what we do when we are alone yet not really alone because we have separated from ourselves to reflect on what we are doing. We are thinking selves, the "two-in-one," to borrow from Hannah Arendt, engaged in silent dialogue with ourselves.[4]

To reflect on our lives and loves we need humility because we may not like what we see. And we need compassion for ourselves because there are limits to what we can understand, what we can do, how much we can give, and what we can bear. Such humility and compassion seem essential in our love for another.

EMOTIONAL POSSIBILITY

"Every love story is a potential grief story," writes Julian Barnes, reflecting on grief after the death of his wife. Maybe when we read a grief story, we are really looking for the love story it was. We want to know what is "emotionally possible," what love can be: "You put together two people who have not been put together before. Sometimes it is like that first attempt to harness a hydrogen balloon to a fire balloon: do you prefer crash and burn, or burn and crash? But sometimes it works, and something new is made, and the world is changed. Then, at some point, sooner or later, for this reason or that, one of them is taken away. And what is taken away is greater than the sum of what was there. This may not be mathematically possible; but it is emotionally possible."[5]

A man I loved in my youth has died of brain cancer. We were in our early twenties when we last saw each other, and I knew very little of his life after that. The memories that lingered over the ensuing decades had congealed into a few images and sounds:

his beautiful tenor voice, the notes of his trumpet soaring to the ceiling as he practiced alone in the college gym, the graveyard we walked through in the dead of a frozen Winnipeg night.

In an effort to cope with the months of cancer treatments, with the fluctuating hope and despair, this man's wife kept a blog. After his death, I became witness to the raw grief of a woman who obviously loved her husband for many years and who was now caught in the grip of the first days of loss. She wrote a public good-bye letter to him. She sifted through the memorabilia and asked friends and family to send her their own memorabilia and share stories of her beloved. For a long time, she was immersed in their shared past, giving free rein to her desire to keep him near.

The frantic archiving of memories will keep this man close to his wife beyond his death. Her love and her memories of him have merged. The misshapen bits of fifty years of life are molding into a coherent story.

I marvel at the strength of human attachment. If the mind wills us to forget in due course, even just enough to let life pull us back to the present and tempt us to think of the future, the body stubbornly insists on its own memorialization. It is remarkable just how localized loss can be, right down to the minutiae of a life. Impossible to forget the lost lover's touch or voice, laughter, handwriting, shape of fingers. Like the bizarre sensations of a phantom limb, the missing body of another can be felt by us, just here or there, as if only a touch away, an hour or a day. We can conjure every scar and wrinkle, every gesture and habit; all our senses indulge in the act of remembrance. The images that our mourning invokes are like fragments of a torn photograph, itemizing random segments of our lives out of order. In this way, the absent is present. Even years after the loss of a loved one—the passage of time seems immaterial—the longing for the beloved conjures up his or her presence with an exceptional immediacy and fullness nearly palpable. This ability of the mind and senses to bring someone back to us is remarkable, our desire making perceptible what has become imaginary.

Barnes calls this the "past-present," an interregnum when the grammar begins to shift and one must speak of the dead loved one in the past tense but at the same time relishes hearing something about her—flashbacks and fresh memories, friends' dreams of her. These "fugitive moments" hold her briefly in the present, pausing both the past-present and the "inevitable slippage into the past historic."[6]

I read the grief stories of those whose loved ones have died and consider the empathy grief invites. Even if we have not experienced loss in quite the same way, another's pain draws us into the experience, perhaps better than any other human emotion. More than happiness, suffering dissolves the borders between us. We understand something of the experience of loss, another's loss reminds us of our own, whether past or lying in wait for us. Paradoxically, suffering makes us feel more alone than ever. Barnes writes that "one grief throws no light upon another"; death is banal and unique, a reality for which we can never prepare.[7] Very like the chronic physical pain that encloses us in a world others cannot enter; the barrier is the pain that prevents us from focusing on anything beyond our own bodies. It is individual pain. Grief is always an individual's grief even if we all will at some point experience it. Perhaps this is the reason we want to know how others experience what we do; there is relief in emotional resonance.

The particulars fade, and loss expands into a shroudlike mist that we are forced to wander through—a generalized condition. Avoiding it may be the reason for our love of distractions and for the speed of our daily lives. We lose, we reinvest in something else that fills the hole, we lose again. Surviving this cycle—flourishing even—might be a matter of recognizing that our longing for what is lost will always be with us, like Barnes's past-present, and of finding something beautiful in the movement of conjuring and laying to rest.

Barnes shares a comment he received from a friend after the death of his wife: "'The thing is—nature is so exact, it hurts exactly as much as it is worth, so in a way one relishes the pain, I think. If it didn't matter, it wouldn't matter.'"[8] Grief takes on the shape of the lost person, loss an affective substitute for the missing body. We are reluctant to part with the grief because it will feel like a second death and a betrayal of what we loved.

There is only one way to accommodate the disjunction between lived time and mourning time, and that is to accept grief's intrusion, never to apologize for the depth of feeling, for its raw, jagged edges. Mourning is, after all, a reminder that we loved and were loved, that *we truly lived*, that we experienced an existence that was not quite ours and not quite another's but something both within and beyond us, greater than the sum of its parts. What better way to honor that existence than to learn to live with its passing, with rivers of tears maybe, but also—in time—with grace.

MOURNING TIME

Mourning keeps its own time, or maybe it takes us out of time. Years ago I became friends with someone whose younger sister had been killed in a car accident. My friend described for me in detail where she was when she received the devastating phone call and how she ran into the streets of Madrid after hanging up, mad with the shock of it. When she told me this, it had been three years after the accident. I remember her look of relief when I said that three years was not a long time. Others were expecting her grief to be over.

Much of what is written about grief makes little sense to me. We are told there are identifiable stages, a linear road back to happiness. Grief appears more wavelike, but without the predictable rhythm we love about the waves of the sea. Each wave threatens to overwhelm; I flap weakly against the force of it, sometimes allow myself to slip under the surface, to escape sound and the unbearable lightness of air. Eventually the waves stop pounding, the water stills. I float quietly for a time until a new wave swells. There is no way to predict how long I will rest undisturbed before the next aftershock brings on the high waves—a moment of solitude, the lyrics of a song, a photograph, or something so mundane as a trip to the grocery store.

There is an expectation from others, especially from those who love us, that time is up. They fear we will not let go; they want to help lift us out of our despondency and feel frustrated when they fail to do so, or they believe our feelings are too intense, out of proportion if the relationship was brief. They lose patience. Grieving people speak of a time when friends stop asking them about the person they loved and lost and of how painful and lonely grief then becomes. Like sole survivors of a disaster, they are alone in the work of remembering and mourning the beloved and the love itself. There is a stubborn loyalty to both the love experienced and the life to which one was deeply attached. We want to speak the names of our loved ones to savor once again that familiar love rolling off the tongue but also to ensure that others will remember. Their forgetting, like our forgetting, feels like a terrible betrayal.

My friend uses the word *surge* to describe my grief: a heavy billowing or swelling motion coming out of nowhere. I imagine a slack, white sail suddenly distended by a gust of wind or the swell of the sea, lifting me effortlessly from its sandy floor. Swollen with sensations from the past, the surge disobeys the rules of time and dredges up old emotions buried in their too-shallow graves. We are pulled into a timeless, soundless, underwater world. This is how my past love visits me—in memories and the stories they become. I am drenched with the sensuality I lost, feeling once again what I felt when I lived in the world of that love. The past is present again. Time as we know it carries no weight; there is only the heaviness of the grief, like rocks in our pockets as we wade deeper and deeper.

My friend assures me: Life will pull you back. You must learn to ride these waves without resisting, trusting in the force of the future—of life and love to come—to lift you above the swell.

And he is right.

COSMIC GIFT

Todd May argues that death saves our love for us. There is a fragility to those we love and to the relationships we have with them. Because they will not always be with us, our time together is particularly meaningful. Places we visit are significant because they are not "infinitely available" to us. The fact that we get old renders this fragility more visible—we are touched by witnessing this aging process in the features of someone we love; it reminds us that we have only so much time with this person. The mortality of not only our lives but also of our loves thus lends an intensity to romantic love that immortality would not allow, taking our loved ones from us yet giving them to us all the more while we and they are here. As such, mortality gives to love an ambivalent "cosmic gift."[9]

Slavoj Žižek considers the other side of this. He tells us that the phone calls made by those who knew they were about to die during the terrorist attacks in the United States on September 11, 2001, were essentially to say "I love you" to their loved ones. This makes intuitive sense to us: at the brink of death contact with those we love, whether for the assurance that we loved or were loved, is what we believe is most important. But Žižek remains suspicious that these confessions of love are opportunistic expressions of fear. Would not the true ethical act be "a wife phoning her husband in the last seconds of her life to tell him: 'Just wanted to let you know that our marriage was a sham, that I cannot stand the sight of you'"?[10]

The event of death or the knowledge of its imminence lends urgency to daily life with the one we love. We stand by the sick or dying, fearful of losing them, bursting with the accumulated love of years and with a confusion of emotions: sorrow, regret, despair, anger. Yet the week before we may have been fighting. Which is the more honest moment? There is no need to choose. It is not about the truth of love, but about the mutability of emotions. That we love someone is as true as anything we feel toward another is true, but within this truth is an expansive affective world that can turn on a dime. To those we love most intimately, we entrust the chaos of our emotions—love mixed with anger, jealousy, resentment, shame, even hatred.

But in the face of death our priorities and preoccupations are rearranged, as anyone knows who has sat in a hospital waiting room. When someone we love undergoes surgery or emergency treatment, and we wait helplessly for an outcome over which we have no control, we know beyond a doubt that we love this person. As May suggests, the fact of mortality intensifies our attachments. In the waiting room, the world seems suddenly in focus, as though we have emerged from a fog of indifference or irrelevance. At this moment, we transcend ourselves. The love becomes bigger than us as we leave ourselves and everything else behind. This does not mean love disappears in other more mundane contexts, as in the middle of a fight, however intense. At those times, we separate; we dwell in our own needs, desires, and wounds—justifiably so and hopefully, honestly. In order to love well, we need to manage—until the limit—these shifts between overcoming and dwelling, joining and separating, loving and hating.

In some instances, Žižek's skepticism might be apt. But I would rather assume that in the face of death love is not an illusion, a betrayal of less-charitable desires, or even an idealization, but rather the lucid recognition of the value of love and of the beloved. The rest is forgiven, swept aside as insignificant, forgettable. And that is probably the point at which we realize that not much else matters in life besides love.

In this sense, May is right to call death a cosmic gift, for it gives meaning to a life, but it also takes that meaning away. We live and love with this ever-present danger. "As soon as I love," Cixous writes, "death is there, it camps out right in the middle of my body," because the need for the beloved is overwhelming: "that's why anguish bursts forth: because the need pushes us toward the realization—that no matter what, yes, I must die."[11]

A student in one of my classes said that there is no point in falling in love because we all are going to die alone. He seemed bitter, perhaps disappointed or disillusioned. We might believe that human mortality means there is no point to anything, love included. But if there is no point to anything, then we are free to make a point of everything—even the seemingly insignificant and unnecessary moments of our lives.

"It is not for nothing we love."[12] It is for everything, from the banal to the sublime. For the exchange of words, for the sound of laughter, for the expression of longing and grief, for touch, for understanding, for the time of remembering and forgetting, for beauty, for idealization and indulgence, for loss and pain and gratitude.

LOSING IS OURS

What do we do with the experience of loss? Mourning may turn into a numbing melancholia after a time. Grief can erupt into grievance, spreading bitterness where it can. The raw pain of being wrenched from what is known and loved might give way to a dull ache. Still, something has to be done with the loss. It has to *go somewhere*. Grief, even forgetting, has a shape.[13] Some will struggle to exorcise it, to purge the pain. Others will carry the loss with them, a weight absorbed into the body that is eventually accepted, cherished even. "Losing is also *ours*," writes Rainer Maria Rilke.[14]

Does this mean we forget? Maybe, in the sense that we let go of that to which we once felt inimitably attached. Life marches on, regardless of whether we want it to. In the words of Francine Niyitegeka, a survivor of the Rwandan genocide in 1994, "We must simply take up life again, since life has so decided." The resilience expressed in these words astonishes me every time I read them. They are spoken by a woman whose baby was killed in her arms. What greater loss can there be?[15]

Intimate himself with such extreme loss, David Grossman explores the work of mourning in *Falling Out of Time*, a novel that defies the borders between poetry and drama as it defies the unspeakable nature of grief. Residents of a town, all of whom have survived the death of a child, embark on a memorializing journey to reach their dead children, encountering one another as they circle the town. The man who begins this walk, simply called "Walking Man," tries to understand the shape of his own grief and this new relation of the living to the dead.

"You are outside of time," Walking Man says to his dead son, and even the sentiment of missing him is trapped in time. Grief ages, as does this man's fury at all that was robbed from his son; the feelings are fresh some days, "but you are no longer," he says, trying to comprehend the event that the words stand in for. As another mourner puts it, talking about his own son who died one August,

> How can I move
> to September
> while he remains
> in August?[16]

I weep over these lines, imagining the unimaginable grief over the finality of death, impossible to comprehend when it is a child, so out of joint with the natural course of things. Children are never supposed to die before their parents; when they do, it is unspeakable, unnatural, beyond anything we might understand or accept. For this is the limit of human acceptance, a limit Grossman consistently evokes in this astounding work. Walking Man says:

I understand, almost,
the meaning of the sounds:
the boy is dead. I recognize
these words as holding truth:
he is dead. I know.
Yes, I admit it: he is dead.
But his death—it swells,
abates,
fulminates.
Unquiet,
unquiet
is his death.
So unquiet.[17]

The "almost" of understanding is echoed in the chorus of walkers who lament with Walking Man the inability to accept the absolute finality of their children's deaths:

WALKING MAN: It can't be that it happened to me,
 it can't be that these words are true—
WALKERS: *It can't be, it can't be—*
WOMAN IN NET: That I saw them throwing my boy into a pit in the earth—
MIDWIFE: That I heard—*thud-thud-thud*—the sound of a hoe digging in the soil—
WALKERS: *It cannot be that these words are true, they cannot be the truth—*
WALKING MAN: It simply cannot be.
MIDWIFE: Burn! Burn the words! Burn this miserable talk![18]

A paradoxical demand, for, as Grossman has said in a public lecture, the consciousness of the disaster that befell him on the death of his son Uri during the second Lebanon war "now permeates every minute" of his life. Memory is powerful and at times paralyzing, he admits, but writing creates a space: "an emotional expanse that I have never known before, where death is more than the absolute, unambiguous opposite of life."[19]

Only in writing, then, can this death have a place, but the finality of the words makes us want to burn them. As though merely seeing the event in print makes it real. The character Centaur in *Falling Out of Time* puts it this way:

Yet still it breaks my heart,
my son,
to think
that I have—
that one could—
that I have found
the words.[20]

There is no finality as absolute as death, but we experience lesser finalities throughout life. Doors that close and cannot be reopened. How intolerable these closed doors can be, and how much more intolerable when we have to shut them ourselves. I cannot forget, I will never forget, the day you asked me, *Are you never coming back?* And how answering you was like breaching the barrier of my ribcage to grip my spleen and pull it out against the will of my body and the laws of nature. Breaking and tearing everything on its way out, this spleen, this word "no." Never say never, the saying goes, alluding to the ever-present possibility of return and repeat. But *never* means the death of possibility and return. Never belongs to the realm of death. How we strain and heave against the never.

Friedrich Nietzsche said, "This is the hardest thing: to close the open hand because one loves."[21] Harder than closing the open hand because one *no longer* loves. Harder because it is unnatural. These experiences of grief share the inconceivable, the incomprehensible, the unspeakable. The time is out of joint when we leave someone we love; it feels as impossible as moving through iron air.

GRIEVING THE LIVING

The books I find on grief are for those whose loved ones have died. They die once, a definitive end without ambiguity that one must, someday, accept or live a lie.

Advice on the grieving process after leaving someone we love is harder to find. The reasons for leaving are always there, but some days they are not good enough, and the longing to return is great. It would be so easy to return. When the person you have lost is not dead, only a small gesture is required to reach out to him. Picking up a phone, sending a message, pressing a few keys on a cell phone, or driving to the old neighborhood. We can remain living in the world created between lovers, reading social network sites, hearing news through friends, replaying in our mind the events of the relationship for months or even years after the leaving.

There are parallels between these experiences of grief, but they are not quite the same. When we leave the person we love, we may never see that dear face again, but what adds to this

unbearable fact is that we *could*. The beloved lives and breathes—
we are mourning not his death, but the dying of the "we." The
umbilical cord must be severed, but because we are not simply
two lives that will be released back into our own orbits once that
cord is cut, with the severance comes the tearing apart of our own
insides. We return amputated to our separate worlds.

We might cling to the remainder, the fragments of a love that
obstinately resists forgetting. The dread of finality, of the irrevocable death of love, keeps us entangled. Alain de Botton gives these
words to the narrator whose lover has just left him for another
man: "Forgetting, however calming, was also a reminder of infidelity to what I had at one time held so dear."[22] There is betrayal
in the burial of a love. Moment by moment, our forgetting seems
to diminish the love we had, like an object that recedes from us
becomes smaller and smaller until it is only a dot on the horizon.
All events in life recede like this, blending into a past until they
are nearly imperceptible as singular events and appear as though
they fit perfectly into a pattern. When we look at a painting up
close, we can isolate a dab of color that seems luminous, pregnant
with purpose, yet nebulous. From a distance, we know that dab is
part of a body or a landscape; we no longer see it distinctly, but as
part of a story. We see the whole picture, as though each distinctive element had its place, its destiny. Old loves become part of
our story. We find a place for them in time.

If our love becomes a past love, bound by a narrative that
begins and ends, we fear it was not as powerful as we once believed
it was. And that can be a terrible thought, perhaps because we
believe for love to be true or pure it must endure forever. For love
to die is so unbearable a thought that we would rather sacrifice a
history of what we thought at the time was an extraordinary love
than admit that love may be powerful and pure and then over.

During a time of intense love, we believe we will always love this person and he will always love us. We may be assured, again and again, with passionate sincerity, "You are the only woman for me, and I will love you forever." Without these assurances, we wonder if love is real.

Yet experience does not bear out that true love must endure forever. The fact that love may end does not deny its truth.

SINGULARITY AND BETRAYAL

In a classroom discussion of the beginnings and ends of love, a student once asked how long it takes before we can love again when it seems we never will. There is no ready answer to this question, and I don't think I gave him one. One person might love again on the heels of the end of love and be criticized for not mourning long enough, for "rebounding," as we like to call it. Another might languish a long time, nursing a slow heart. Move on, his friends may say. It is enough.

In an unusual chapter of *Love's Knowledge*, Martha Nussbaum's narrator is falling in love with someone new in the wake of the death of a previous love, which inspires a discussion of what is individual in love and what might be universal or repeatable. The singularity of love has to do with a person's idiosyncratic characteristics; these properties are unique, nonrepeatable. But Nussbaum believes there are universal elements in any love; the values or aspirations loved in one person might be repeated in another. The death of one love might mean the birth of a new love for a person who shares these values. To illustrate this claim, Nussbaum's narrator reflects on the diary of the early-twentieth-century painter Dora Carrington. After the death of her beloved,

Lytton Strachey, Carrington complains about well-intentioned friends who insist she will love again. Seeking to comfort her, they assure her that certain general features of Lytton might be found in someone else, values and aspirations that Carrington could continue to love and cherish even if they were not realized in a particular life.[23]

Nussbaum's narrator concludes that it would be an excellent result for Carrington's grief if a richer love of the individual turned out to be based on an acknowledgment that some things have an intrinsic value and are repeatable, meaning that they will survive the death or departure of an individual and might be located in another. The "better" one loved this individual, the more one would see that there was something to live for beyond that person, connected with the commitments and aspirations on which the love was based. "To survive the death of love is not just logically possible but also morally best," Nussbaum notes. Furthermore, "the best conception of love is one that permits some sort of replacement of individuals." But the narrator warns: be on your guard; this argument may be shaped by the fact that I have just been writing a love letter to someone new.[24] In other words, the narrator might be seeking only to justify her replacement of the old love with a new one. We are attached to our belief in enduring love and dislike admitting to its death; we may feel guilt in admitting to a new love. There is consolation in this reincarnation of love, in this transgression of limits.

We do not really fall in love with values, though. Otherwise, as Todd May points out, we would love all those who share those values, but we don't.[25] We love particular persons, and we love certain values and privilege certain aspirations, but these persons and these values do not always coincide. What we witness here is the search for something enduring to console us in the face of limits. Nussbaum reaffirms that in the moral order of things enduring love (not necessarily with only one person) is the only love worth having, the only good love.

I want to object: we do not love replacements. Every love is individual and needs to be recognized as such. *Who we are* every time we love is singular, summoned into being by the love itself; the love that draws us into the life and love of another. This is why our dearest friends may not be dear to each other. Each one loves the singular in us with the singular in him or her to which another friend would have no access. We go beyond ourselves to create something between two that another could not share and do this multiple times. Every friend, every love inspires a new configuration impossible to replicate.

We can be grateful to this sheer individuality, then, for the infinite possibilities of love. We can always love again. Tomorrow maybe or the day after. And it will be unlike any other love that passed before.

There is another outcome to the passing of each unique love. At the end of love, we reverse the process of the beginning of love. The two worlds that collided and overlapped, creating a unique third space, the interworld of two, is now divided. But the two do not return to the worlds they inhabited previously because they have adapted, transformed their shape to accommodate another shape. Each of them is irrevocably altered. As they move apart, they take with them their own stories of a shared life, for no one has precisely the same story as another, even the closest of lovers. And this is where betrayal sneaks in, either unbidden or intended by the resentful one. There is no way to avoid this act of betrayal and the guilt it instigates because what was once the private world between two, with its accumulation of shared stories, is splintered. Lovers cease to protect that privacy and need or want to be true to what have become their own stories.

The past love no longer looks the same in this new separated state, and neither does the story. As time goes by, this change becomes more noticeable. Years later, when we meet our former lovers, we might be surprised that we ever loved them to begin with. This does not mean we should not have loved them or that they were not "right" for us. It only means that we were who we were *because* we were together. And now that we are separate, we have become other than who we were when we were together. If we love again, we will become someone new in the new relation to another.

THE AMBIGUITY OF LONELINESS

Loneliness is as fundamental to the human condition as love. We run from one into the arms of the other and sometimes back again. Who does not crave the love that will banish loneliness? We flee loneliness; we fear it, deny it. When we succumb to it, we do not speak of it, as though admitting to loneliness announces something shameful about us. Rarely do we reflect on the social conditions—the norms and imperatives, especially those surrounding coupledom—that give rise to loneliness, believing instead that there must be something wrong with us.

To be alone is not necessarily to be lonely. Solitude might be experienced as a welcome respite—liberating after an exhausting relationship, an exquisite freedom from complicated entanglements. The creative or contemplative person may desire and require more of this stillness than the average person. Too much of it might lead to loneliness, although we can also feel intensely lonely in a crowd, in a family, or in a marriage. Hannah Arendt elaborated the distinction in this way: in solitude I am together with myself, as though I were two, in conversation, but I am only one in loneliness, "deserted by all others."[26]

We experience loneliness as something unnatural, and yet who has never felt lonely? It is one of the fundamental experiences of human life, Arendt notes, and yet it is contrary to the basic requirements of the human condition. Every aspect of human life depends on our being in contact with others, inhabiting shared spaces, communicating, caring, interacting. When we are deprived of this togetherness, we cease to have a place in the world that is recognized and guaranteed by others. We become superfluous, which means, according to Arendt, that we do not belong to the world at all.[27]

Loneliness has many faces. There is the loneliness after losing someone who occupied a place in the center of our existence, on whom we relied for daily human contact and conversation, whose absence leaves a hole that no one else seems able to fill. This loneliness is a painful lack, gnawing on the inside like hunger. There is the loneliness of emotional or psychological isolation when we do not feel close enough to anyone, whether we are surrounded by people or alone. This is a loneliness that social activities do not mitigate, for what we long for is a deep exchange. Aging inaugurates another kind of loneliness: the new invisibility of being forgotten or neglected, and the loss not only of a companion but also of the work and care that gave our life meaning. There is the loneliness of living alone, oppressed by the stillness, by the obstinately silent objects that surround us, and by time, stretching out intolerably as we wish for the sleep of night to banish our loneliness.

A painful longing is present in all of these manifestations of loneliness. We might feel as though we are living in a bubble; no one can touch us or see us, and no one hears us. We are abandoned by the world, or the world has disappeared, and we are alone. It may feel like an intentional act of cruelty against us, a kind of death by exclusion; the world audaciously continues without us.

There is desire in those of us who are lonely, but that desire is contingent on how each one of us traverses that ultimate barrier between one being and another. Some require the comforting sounds of another person in our home or on the other side of shared walls or the reassuring touch of hands, the intimacy of skin on skin. Others might need the kind of conversation we have in the dead of night when the darkness obliterates anything resembling distance between lovers. There are only disembodied voices tripping over each other, merging words, sentiments, ideas— neither knows where one ends and the other begins. Still others may want only the soothing chatter that rises over the hedges of our neighbor's yard, that flows across the counter at our local café or in the crowded bar at the end of the day. All of these things speak to individual social needs—to belong to one another, to slip in and out of another's life even if our days overlap only momentarily, over coffee, over tears or laughter or passion. These encounters pull us out of our solitary selves and in the best of possible worlds return us to them—but not to lonely selves. We return alone but not lonely, alone yet taking with us something of these others—bits of conversations, images of beloved faces, fragments of ideas or residues of emotions. The intensity of the conversation, the electricity of skin, the kind words across a hedge, nurture what lies between us—something shared, something beyond either of us and yet possible only through our exchange.

Vivian Gormick writes of sitting down to dinner by herself in her New York City apartment, comforted by the life outside her windows. "My mind flashes on all who crossed my path today," she explains, "I hear their voices, I see their gestures, I start filling in lives for them. Soon they are company, great company."[28] In the big city, there are always people, and even if we do not know them, there is comfort in being surrounded by human life, by people on the street on a Saturday morning or in the cafés at any time. The sheer volume means that there is nothing truly unusual, certainly not the solitary person. I read of Gormick's pleasure in the "archaeology" of New York City voices and think of one of the loneliest times of my life, staying in a Berlin apartment complex in early winter, where I took comfort in the lights coming from the windows around me, in the glimpse of others' daily lives as they read by evening lamplight or cooked dinner together.

The most devastating loneliness, I imagine, would result from living without at least some form of human exchange—of minds, skin, words, emotion, ideas, or idle chatter—and in the complete absence of love. This would mean living inside the walls of an absolutely separate and impenetrable self. Lovelessness is the essence of the worst kind of loneliness.

SURVIVAL

I was at war with myself and with your embattled psyche, anticipating the death of our "we" despite loving in the most intense manner I had ever known. For several months, I lived on the edges of dread, both admitting and denying that this death was approaching and that I would have to survive it, afraid of the finality that would be the result of this leaving. Fearing, above all, the abyss of loneliness and loss, of the absence I knew I would feel keenly. Wondering how I would survive, overcome by the fear that *you* would not survive, despite knowing without knowing that your survival demanded my departure, that you were, through the thick wall of my denial, begging me to leave.

With this survival on my mind, I read Jacques Derrida's final interview, printed in *Le Monde* on August 19, 2004, some two months before he died of cancer, alongside Gillian Rose's memoir, *Love's Work: A Reckoning with Life.* These texts could come only from the dying: more manifesto than meditation, they rail against what Derrida calls the rapidly shrinking period of deferral. There is a raw urgency to their pronouncements and a refusal of what Rose calls "repose." Life is lived in the theater of the agon, in revel, on the edge, as love is also lived. For neither life nor love are exceptional, Rose writes; "To live, to love, is to be failed."[29] We find Derrida's version of the agon in his famous line "I am at war with myself."[30] And so Rose remains faithful to the epigraph of her bold memoir—"Keep your mind in hell, and despair not"— and Derrida follows close behind—"I have never learned . . . to accept death."[31]

In answer to his interviewer's question, Derrida emphatically states that, no, he has not learned how to live, for learning how to live means learning how to die—to acknowledge and accept absolute mortality without resurrection or redemption. "I have never learned . . . to accept death," Derrida protests, and "I remain uneducable when it comes to . . . knowing-how-to-die." He believes in the truth of this relation between taking death into account and learning to live, but he cannot resign himself to it because it would mean rejecting what he loves.[32]

It is common to think that we can live our lives well only in the full awareness of death, that we must be resigned to it. Derrida's persistent attention to the difference that interrupts all absolutes—such as life or death—and to the fact that each concept is tainted by its other might lend itself to this viewpoint. There is no life without death; there is no conceivable understanding of life that excludes death. We could call it *lifedeath* or *living death*, for death intrudes on life at every moment, through dying skin cells and aging organs, the prospect of disease or disaster, and the painful encroachment of a sense of finality. But the acceptance of life's absolute limit does not allow us to live at peace with ourselves or perfect our lives. Derrida as a dying man refuses this interpretation, affirming the idea of life as survival, as living after death—over or beyond death, in excess of death. Survival "is not derived from either living or dying"—no more than "a mourning that does not wait for the so-called 'actual' death."[33]

Rose and Derrida tell us something about survival in the doubled meaning provided by the German terms *fortleben* and *überleben*, "living on" and "living through." That is, living on in what remains, consoled by life beyond death (or life over life as the term *sur-vie* implies), as opposed to living through or enduring. Survival as endurance (*überleben*) essentially refuses the consolation of survival as living beyond (*fortleben*), as these dying philosophers will show us.[34]

But to say that we do not learn how to live means only that we do not learn how to live *finally*—that is, definitively. In these liberal times, our social imperative is to learn how to live and how to love best, *finally*. We are instructed in the art of living: how to eat, exercise, save money, grow old, perfect our own and our children's lives. We search for the perfect love relationships to ensure maximum happiness, and we solicit the help of therapists when we do not find them. Happiness is equated with perfection and a kind of clean normalcy. In our pristine love relationships, we believe that love does not—*cannot*—end. The promise of love *is* its immortality. So we love while refusing love's death, imminent or eventual. In fact, we refuse to entertain the merest thought that love might die. We believe that love overflows us, infinitely larger and more powerful than we are when we love, and to renounce this belief is to ask love to die. If love is stronger than the lover, it will live on even after the death of the lovers—this is evidence of our "love-preservation" instinct. So lovers are buried side by side, and love letters—like those between Abelard and Héloise—are the remainders (traces, Derrida might say) of a great love, immortalized. At weddings, lovers promise to love forever. When the marriage ends in divorce, people say it could not have been love to begin with—at least, not *true love*. We live our loves as though love will never die.

Life is not perfectible, and neither is love. We do not learn anything definitively, but only conditionally and partially because life is always unfinished. We are spared arrival, as Hélène Cixous puts it, and happily so: "I want arriv*ance*, movement, unfinishing in my life," she writes, "to depart (so as) not to arrive."[35] We *move* in life—or rather, life moves us—we do not learn in the sense of finally arriving. And we could say the same of love.

The impulse to survive death and, more, to insist that we *will* survive it is captured by the term *fortleben*—something survives a death and lives on, and this living on appears to be our only consolation in the face of insignificance and fungibility. When forced to acknowledge the absolute limit of death, we strive to establish a legacy, any type of offspring that will extend our life beyond death: the books, ideas, art, or children to which we give birth. And love. Derrida says,

One wants to live as much as possible, to save oneself, to persevere, and to cultivate all these things which, though infinitely greater and more powerful than oneself, nonetheless form a part of this little "me" that they exceed on all sides. To ask me to renounce what formed me, *what I've loved so much*, what has been my law, is to ask me to die. In this fidelity there is a sort of instinct for self-preservation. To renounce, for example, some difficult formulation, some complication, paradox, or supplementary contradiction . . . is for me an unacceptable obscenity.[36]

The legacy of life in this passage is love. To preserve life is to preserve love—love for ideas, for language, for what has formed us, for what we have created. To be asked to disavow love is to ask us to die; the life-preservation instinct and the love-preservation instinct are one and the same.

Derrida admits to an obsession with inheritance and with his own legacy; he thinks "immodestly" that no one has yet begun to read him and worries that after his death *"there will be nothing left."*[37] The life-preservation instinct is narcissistic, of course; the fidelity of which he speaks is a fidelity to our own significance. Derrida frets over "who is going to inherit, and how? Will there even be any heirs?" Our hope of surviving thanks to this legacy or trace is not "a striving for immortality," he insists; "it is something structural," but the two are not mutually exclusive.[38] Does he protest too much? For what is *sur-vie* in the sense of *fortleben* but a kind of consolation, insulating us from our own insignificance and replaceability? Is this not what we most fear about the death of love? That our love will be forgotten—that *we* will be forgotten; that there will be nothing left, no trace of our presence in the lover's life; that we will be replaced by another and life will go on as though every word, gesture, every touch never happened?

We want to be assured that the love we gave to our lovers or to our children and our friends will live on. So we give our gifts of love, we catalog our loves with memorabilia, we mourn and create, we write our love stories.

Survival is a concept that transcends limits. But Derrida also affirms life unconditionally, *within* its limits. This is "the affirmation of a living being who prefers living and thus surviving to death, because survival is *not simply that which remains* but the most intense life possible."[39] We find in this passage a reference to both senses of survival, for it is not simply a remainder, thus not only a living on, but also a living through. This is the meaning of survival that we find in Rose's text, a survival without consolation. Rose refuses solace, both as a woman dying of cancer and as a woman who has lost a particularly intense love to indifference.

Rose's testaments to the enigmatic lives that populate her memoir—and to her own life—say much about survival as a stubborn resistance not only to mortality but also to the promise of immortality. Here *überleben* refuses the solace of *fortleben*. To learn how to die—and therefore how to live—would entail resignation, settling into a kind of dead life, ironically because to accept the consolation of living on is to ask for a deathless life. Rose refuses this settling, as does Derrida when he invokes the term *negotiation* in the fullness of its etymological meaning: *negotium*, "not-ease," "not-quiet," "no-leisure." When he thinks of negotiation, he says, he thinks "of this without-rest, this enervating mobility preventing one from ever stopping."[40]

There is no living beyond one's limits, but there is a way to live within them, without rest or resignation. Limits enable life even if we hate them. In her new cancerous life, Rose discovers that what others find most daunting is not her illness or possible death but her "accentuated being; not [her] morbidity, but [her] renewed vitality." This is the enigmatic paradox of living most intensely, most vitally, and without rest while dying and while refusing any consolation. Rose gives us an injunction that she strangely refers to as "dying forward" rather than "dying deadly." We "die forward into the intensified agon of living" rather than accept the deathless, limitless life of happiness and perfectibility. Devastated by the loss of her great love for Father Patrick, she declares, "Let me then be destroyed. For that is the only way I may have a chance of surviving. . . . Now I am not dissociated from my ululation. I hear the roaring and the roasting and know that it is I."[41]

Rose and Derrida—two brilliant, passionate individuals fighting against limits while succumbing to them. Death is inextricable from life, and yet we refuse it and must refuse it in order to live forward rather than to live deadly, to twist Rose's formulation. We want immortality—if our bodies cannot live forever, then our work can, or our love can. If love does not endure a lifetime, then it lives on in a subsequent love. Or we immortalize a dead love by telling its story, turning tragedy into beauty, and by doing so we mitigate the pain of finality and loss. This resistance to limits lends an intensity to life that we would not otherwise experience. We fight with our limits because we are greedy for life, as we are greedy for love and for the significance and meaning it provides us.

Life, love, and death converge in this lust for survival. We mourn ourselves in the anticipation of being forgotten in a world that audaciously continues after our lives come to an end. Derrida says in "Circumfession," "I see myself dead cut off from you in your memories that I love and I weep like my own children at the edge of my grave."[42] Part of this mourning is the justification of our lives and loves that we seem compelled to make.

So we elaborate the idea that death and life are not absolutes, and we create concepts such as "living death" or "dying forward," and we read Rose, Cixous, or Derrida to affirm our own patterns in love and life. We may cling to the idea that immortality would lead to an edgeless love or a life of passivity or repose without intensity to justify our own struggle in the "intensified agon of living" that enabled us to live and to love. Those who choose the repose rather than the revel will elaborate their own justifications.

What does this mean for our past loves? Our lost or dying loves? There is survival in the sense of living on at the end of love, for physical separation, even through death, may not mean the absence of the beloved. Our lost loves continue to inhabit us, and not just in our memories: they have helped to create who we are.

There is also survival as living through or "dying forward." To love is to affirm the agonistic elements that intensify love and to refuse the consolation of happy love. After surgery performed to assess the progression of her cancer, Rose's surgeon tells her, "You are living in symbiosis with the disease. Go away and continue to do so." And this is precisely what Rose does when she invents a "colostomy ethnography" to describe her relation to her own excrement, "uniform, sweet-smelling fruit of the body" hanging hot in a bag flush with her abdomen. "I handle my shit" she writes, "I no longer employ the word as an expletive, discharging intense, momentary irritation into its void of meaning."[43] In love we live in symbiosis with disease, for love is neither clean nor perfectible—and we must learn to *handle our shit*. There may be remainders, but these traces also eventually die. We refuse to accept this—we will go on mourning our own deaths and our own loves as though the only thing that matters is to survive them. We will go on seeking consolation in what overcomes our limits.

To live in symbiosis with the disease and despair not? In life as in love, we are "insensible of mortality" and yet "desperately mortal," as Rose wisely observes.[44] There is no "should" in this conclusion, no best love to recommend or instruction on how to live and love well. Only a refusal to judge a love as failed, only a rejection of consolation.

MONUMENTS

It was only a room, but it drew breath in my presence and sighed when I left. An oasis of light and green, branches tapping the windows as I wrote. Those trees I have not forgotten; silent witnesses to weeping, our rapport a casualty of history.

The walls of that room I meant to paint—a Salvadoran yellow to remind me of a garden I once had, of lime and eucalyptus trees, of bougainvillea, bracing under a hot sun. There was always a future in that room, and hope. There was love.

When all was bare, the light turned, exposing the ruins of desertion: a paper clip and crumpled grocery list, a sticky-note heart. Monuments to life lived, banalities forgotten, caught in dust balls here and there on the hardwood.

The clock was still, the books gone. We might have shared their lines across the clutter one day, to break the solitude of thinking. And laughed or sighed, assured of understanding.

Those old panes and the green beyond that nourished my morning eyes will be there tomorrow and then tomorrow, my absence unremarked, time and beauty regardless.

AFTERWORD

I READ the lines I have written here and everywhere sense the impressions left by my friends, their thoughts like hands around my own, coaxing form and shape out of unwieldy material. When we lose a person with whom we have built an intimate world, the circumference of privacy must expand. We always need more than one. Only in a social milieu that prizes coupledom at the expense of all other relationships, including community itself, do we obscure this fact. How full our lives can be, how enriched, when we accept both the pleasure and the ache of the vulnerability that flows between us thanks to our need for one another.

No one would choose to live without friends, says Aristotle in *Nicomachean Ethics*.[1] Even those who seem to have it all need friends; the wealthy and the powerful need them more than anyone, for what is prosperity without the opportunity of beneficence? Who would help them protect their wealth and power? Friends are essential, too, for those who suffer the misery of poverty and misfortune, for friends provide refuge. The young require friends to keep them from error, and the old rely on friends to help meet increasing needs, while those in the prime of life need friends to stimulate thinking and acting. Friendship, Aristotle believes—"when two go together"—is familiar to parents and their offspring, to animals and birds, and to the different human races. Even states appear to be held together by friendship, he remarks, and lawgivers care more for it than justice, for "if people are friends, they have no need of justice."[2]

Friendship is not only necessary, according to Aristotle, but a very fine thing. The best friendship is based on virtue—friends prove themselves good and trustworthy, the conditions he finds necessary for being lovable. But such friendships are rare; they require a great deal of time and emotional investment. Ideal friendship means a person is loved for herself, not instrumentally or selfishly for the pleasure the friend provides. Becoming friends with someone merely for what he or she can give to us will prove dissatisfying, Aristotle warns; instrumental friendships do not endure.[3] He could not have anticipated the superficial forms of "friending" sought in our times, feeding narcissism and the longing for significance and connection through channels that demand almost nothing from us. We seek ever wider circles of friends and dilute the meaning of friendship. For what reason? What do we escape in the dilution? Vulnerability and the sacrifice of our own needs, pain sometimes, the demands of care, but also a meaningful life.

The difference between the love we bear for a friend and the love we share with an intimate partner is generally thought to depend on sexual activity, although this distinction has recently come into question with interest in polyamorous or "friends with benefits" couplings. But sex alone does not constitute the line between friends and lovers. Relationships move along a spectrum of intimacy and intensity, which means we grant different priorities to the people we love. We would drop everything to rush to the hospital bedside of a spouse or lover or one of our closest friends, but perhaps not for an acquaintance or colleague. We spend our days off, our holidays or special occasions, with those we love the most, those with whom we can be most ourselves, most vulnerable, most familiar, most relaxed. We are not "at home" with everyone. How could we be? The emotional intensity of such closeness requires time and devotion. With our friends we might avoid the conflicts that arise in a more intimate relationship. There is more "space" between friends than between intimate partners. The closer we are in emotional or psychological proximity to someone (which usually means physical proximity as well), the more vulnerable we are to the loved one's fluctuating emotions and to hurting and being hurt. We negotiate our friends' and lovers' peculiarities or weaknesses to varying degrees.

This negotiation tells us something about the unavoidable and necessary movement between binding and separating in any two individuals who love each other. Friendship love might allow us to think about more intimate love in a way that escapes some of the latter's mythical proportions. Our building of friendships is less prescribed. We tend not to feel as though a new friendship we develop *must* last a lifetime or is not worth our effort. We do not make a legal commitment, plan a religious ceremony, or draw up a contract. Our dedication to the friendship is motivated by something else. First, enjoyment of the other's company. I would call this enjoyment the eros of friendship, a kind of lust not for sexual arousal and satisfaction, but for a friend's presence and rapport and for the effects of communion with her or him—Simone de Beauvoir's "delicious 'we'"[4]—a sense of solidarity and belonging that lingers long after we part. Friends create an interworld similar to that of the intimate couple, for two friends together generate something between them that is utterly unique.

I treasure my running conversations with friends, conversations that have now spanned years, but with each friend the rapport is distinctive. I may tell them similar tales of my cares and concerns on any given day, but from each friend I receive a different response, generating new insights and perspectives. We shape each other uniquely when we are together.

The pleasure of time spent in the company of these friends is immeasurable—hours in which we slide with ease from childhood memories to future anxieties, from the books and films we love to the terrors of the world and the challenges of parenting, teaching, or writing. We trip over each other's words, racing along the paths of our thoughts like children on bicycles. For me, this eros of friendship is inseparable from the eros of the life of the mind. I think and feel together with my friends. As we talk, we create, we make discoveries, we analyze our dreams, our experiences, and the ideas of our best-loved thinkers, attempting together to understand both the banal and the profound. We inspire and move one another—to tears or laughter or contemplation. Without each other, there would be no understanding, only the stasis of a solitary mind. Without friends, we would live a worldless, empty existence.

It catches me by surprise to discover my friends love me simply for who I am. This is not love for what I can give to them, but love for me as a *person*, a presence in the world who was encountered by chance. In this love is the affirmation we find in Augustine's expression "volo ut sis"—my friends affirm me without reason, inexplicably, not on account of any particular feature or quality. They love *who* I am, not *what* I am. In this affirmation, we find respect above all, accompanied by kindness and care. Out of respect, we are careful—we know one another's sore spots and when compassion must rise above any other consideration.

I sense when I tax my friends, but this is when I feel their respect most keenly. Kindness tempers impatience or irritation when we love someone with respect for his or her person. Not everything needs to be said—we allow each other to separate and come together again. Friendship is not without the risk of pain, disagreement, and loss, as in any love relationship, but the profound respect we find in the affirmation of "volo ut sis" helps us accept one another's limits.

There is no violence in my friendship loves. But with the greatest intimacy comes the greatest risk of violence. In friendship love, we give up both, and sometimes in the course of our lives this is what we need. Not to fall asleep in another's arms, but not to feel a lover's anger either, not to delve too deeply into another's unconscious.

The generosity my closest friends show me is greater than what I have experienced in my most intimate relationships. This is not to make a universal claim about friendship love but to acknowledge that the love from friends *can be* far more sustaining than we might realize. Social scripts being what they are, the intimate other is overburdened with demand and too often given the responsibility for our well-being. We are reticent (or even ashamed) to recognize how much we need our friends and to freely acknowledge this need. But this world of need, generosity, and kindness is part of the delight of friendship. We know we need one another; the need provokes us to love generously, and this giving adds to the pleasure of our rapport. We are augmented by our mutual love and the desire to be in one another's company. We feel most ourselves; we feel at home.

To be involved in another's life—deeply involved—is a privilege none of us should turn down. We have little choice in the form these involvements take. Love relationships always arise out of a moment of chance, and we must live our lives in openness to the luck of our encounters—holding open our hands to grasp another's, never knowing what this person will become to us. I think of the first time I met each of my closest friends and marvel at the chance confluence of our histories, at the instant affinity arising out of a sense that here before me stands a kindred spirit. This is one of life's great gifts. We need the tangled connections that may develop, connections that are sometimes comforting, at other times exhausting. The breaks and the reunions, the disappointment and the forgiveness—these are what give our lives meaning, these give us stories to tell.

The worst loneliness may come not from the lack of *being loved*, but from having no one *to love*. Fortunately, we have the power to overcome this predicament, for there is always someone nearby who needs love.

NOTES

PREFACE

1. Margaret Atwood, *Alias Grace* (Toronto: McClelland & Stewart, 1996), 298.
2. Alexander Herzen, *My Past and Thoughts: The Memoirs of Alexander Herzen*, trans. Constance Garnett, abridged ed. (New York: Knopf, 1973), v, quoted in Gillian Rose, *Love's Work: A Reckoning with Life* (New York: New York Review of Books, 1995), 120.
3. Hélène Cixous and Mireille Calle-Gruber, *Rootprints: Memory and Life Writing*, trans. Eric Prenowitz (New York: Routledge, 1997), 12, 57, 18, 4, 3.
4. Anne Carson, *Eros the Bittersweet* (London: Dalkey Archive Press, 1998), xi–xii; the Kafka story she discusses is "The Top."
5. Tim Lilburn, *Living in the World as If It Were Home: Essays* (Dunvegan, Canada: Cormorant Books, 1999), 89.
6. "Keep your mind in hell, and despair not" is a famous aphorism by Saint Staretz Silouan and the book epigraph of Rose, *Love's Work*.
7. Quoted in Colm Tóibín, "Roaming the Greenwood," *London Review of Books* 29, no. 2 (1999): 12–16, http://www.lrb.co.uk/v21/n02/colm-toibin/roaming-the-greenwood.
8. David Grossman, *Falling Out of Time*, trans. Jessica Cohen (Toronto: McClelland & Stewart, 2014), 77, 87.
9. Cixous and Calle-Gruber, *Rootprints*, 77.

PART I. LEGACY

1. Hélène Cixous, *"Coming to Writing" and Other Essays*, ed. Deborah Jenson, trans. Sarah Cornell, Deborah Jenson, Ann Liddle, and Susan Sellers (Cambridge, Mass.: Harvard University Press, 1991), 39.

2. Abelard, "Letter III," in *The Love Letters of Abelard and Héloise* (London: Dent, 1901), 49, http://sacred-texts.com/chr/aah/index.htm.

3. Irving Singer, "Appraisal and Bestowal," in *The Nature of Love*, vol. 1: *Plato to Luther*, 2nd ed. (Chicago: University of Chicago Press, 1984), 3–22.

4. Alain de Botton, *Essays in Love* (London: Picador, 2006), 202.

5. Singer, "Appraisal and Bestowal," 1:7.

6. Michel Foucault established the relation between prohibition and incitement in *The History of Sexuality: An Introduction*, trans. Robert Hurley (New York: Random House, 1978). He writes of the production of "specific effects on desire" when it is deliberately transformed into discourse: "effects of mastery and detachment, to be sure, but also an effect of spiritual reconversion, of turning back to God, a physical effect of blissful suffering from feeling in one's body the pangs of temptation and the love that resists it" (23).

7. For verses from the Bible, I use *The New Oxford Annotated Bible*, Revised Standard Version, ed. Herbert G. May and Bruce M. Metzger (New York: Oxford University Press, 1962).

8. Flannery O'Connor, "A Temple of the Holy Ghost," in *A Good Man Is Hard to Find, and Other Stories* (New York: Harcourt, 1955), 88. O'Connor writes: "I am a Temple of the Holy Ghost, she said to herself, and was pleased with the phrase. It made her feel as if somebody had given her a present."

9. Miriam Toews, *All My Puny Sorrows* (Toronto: Knopf, 2014), 251.

10. Jacques Derrida suggests this story exemplifies a conjugal model of hospitality, "paternal and phallogocentric," that transcends ethical obligations and by doing so subjects others—Lot's daughters in this case—to "the violence of the power of hospitality." But it would seem that the exchange of Lot's daughters is at the very heart of hospitality, their sacrifice an ethical obligation in itself from the perspective of

"the familial despot" (*Of Hospitality*, trans. Rachel Bowlby [Stanford: Stanford University Press, 2000], 149–155).

11. Hannah Arendt, *Love and Saint Augustine*, ed. Joanna Vecchiarelli Scott and Judith Chelius Stark (Chicago: University of Chicago Press, 1996), 18.

12. Jean-Paul Sartre, *Being and Nothingness*, trans. Hazel E. Barnes (New York: Washington Square Press, 1993), 481.

13. Susan Sontag, *As Consciousness Is Harnessed to Flesh: Journals and Notebooks, 1964–1980*, ed. David Rieff (New York: Farrar, Straus and Giroux, 2012), 264.

14. Colm Tóibín, *The Testament of Mary* (Toronto: McClelland & Stewart, 2012), 86.

15. Virginia Woolf, *To The Lighthouse* (London: Grafton Books, 1977), 38–39, 42.

16. Teresa of Ávila, *The Life of Teresa of Jesus: The Autobiography of Teresa of Ávila*, trans. and ed. E. Allison Peers (New York: Doubleday, 1991), 274–275.

17. World Health Organization, *Female Genital Mutilation Fact Sheet*, updated February 2014, http://www.who.int/mediacentre/factsheets/fs241/en/.

18. Julia Kristeva, *Tales of Love*, trans. Leon S. Roudiez (New York: Columbia University Press, 1987), 8.

19. Luce Irigaray, "Sorcerer Love, a Reading of Plato's *Symposium*, Diotima's Speech," trans. Eleanor H. Kuykendall, *Hypatia* 3, no. 3 (1989): 32.

20. Plato, *Symposium*, trans. Alexander Nehemas and Paul Woodruff (Indianapolis, Ind.: Hackett, 1989), 181b, 186d.

21. Ibid., 192b–192c.

22. Ibid., 210b, 211e, 210d.

23. This is Irigaray's interpretation in "Sorcerer Love."

24. Plato, *Symposium*, 209c.

25. Ibid., 211a, emphasis in original.

26. Henry Chadwick, introduction to Augustine, *Confessions*, trans. Henry Chadwick (Oxford: Oxford University Press, 1991), xiii.

27. Augustine, *Confessions*, VI.xv.25, VI.xv.25, III.ii.3.

28. Ibid., II.i.1, II.i.1–2, II.iii.6, II.iii.8.

29. Abelard, "Letter I," in *Love Letters*, 8, 6.
30. Abelard, "Letter III," in *Love Letters*, 10, 13–17, 52.
31. Ibid., 42, 46.
32. Ibid., 45, 43, 58, 44.
33. Ibid., 43–45, 48, 49.
34. Ibid., 54, 58.
35. Héloise, "Letter II," in *Love Letters*, 29.
36. Immanuel Kant, "The Doctrine of Virtue," part III of *The Metaphysics of Morals*, trans. Mary J. Gregor (Cambridge: Cambridge University Press, 1996), Akad. 500-1, para. 447 ff., cited in Martha Nussbaum, "Steerforth's Arm: Love and the Moral Point of View," in *Love's Knowledge: Essays on Philosophy and Literature* (Oxford: Oxford University Press, 1990), see 336–337 n. 3.
37. Nussbaum, "Steerforth's Arm," 336–337.
38. Jean-Luc Marion, *The Erotic Phenomenon*, trans. Stephen E. Lewis (Chicago: University of Chicago Press, 2007), 1.
39. Ibid., 3.
40. Ibid., 10, 222.
41. Luce Irigaray writes that woman's sexual organ "represents *the horror of nothing to see*" (*This Sex Which Is Not One*, trans. Catherine Porter with Carolyn Burke [Ithaca: Cornell University Press, 1977], 26).

PART II. LOVE

1. Gillian Rose, *Love's Work: A Reckoning with Life* (New York: New York Review of Books, 1995), 105–106.
2. Hélène Cixous, "Tancredi Continues," in *"Coming to Writing" and Other Essays*, ed. Deborah Jenson, trans. Sarah Cornell, Deborah Jenson, Ann Liddle, and Susan Sellers (Cambridge, Mass.: Harvard University Press, 1991), 79.
3. See Sappho, "Fragments 38, 47, 48, and 130," in *If Not, Winter: Fragments of Sappho*, trans. Anne Carson (New York: Vintage, 2003), 77, 99, 101, 265.
4. Sappho, "Fragment 105a," quoted in Anne Carson, *Eros the Bittersweet* (London: Dalkey Archive Press, 1998), 26, suspension points in original.
5. Carson, *Eros the Bittersweet*, 27, 29, 26.

6. Sappho, "Fragment 31," quoted in Carson, *Eros the Bittersweet*, 12–13.

7. Carson, *Eros the Bittersweet*, 16.

8. Sappho, "Fragment 94," in *If Not, Winter*, 185.

9. Susan Sontag, *As Consciousness Is Harnessed to Flesh: Journals and Notebooks, 1964–1980*, ed. David Rieff (New York: Farrar Straus and Giroux, 2012), 268, bracketed insertion in the original.

10. Toni Morrison, *Beloved* (New York: Penguin Books, 1987), 213.

11. Rose, *Love's Work*, 73.

12. Sappho, "Fragment 130," in *If Not, Winter*, 265.

13. Hannah Arendt, *Love and Saint Augustine*, ed. Joanna Vecchiarelli Scott and Judith Chelius Stark (Chicago: University of Chicago Press, 1996), 9, 19.

14. Carson, *Eros the Bittersweet*, xi.

15. Héloise, "Letter II," in *The Love Letters of Abelard and Héloise* (London: Dent, 1901), 39, 40, http://www.sacred-texts.com/chr/aah/index.htm.

16. Héloise, "Letter V," in *Love Letters*, 83, 82.

17. Héloise, "Letter II," 36.

18. Héloise, "Letter IV," in *Love Letters*, 66.

19. Héloise, "Letter II," 36–37.

20. Rose, *Love's Work*, 69.

21. Sontag, *As Consciousness Is Harnessed to Flesh*, 268–269.

22. M. C. Dillon, *Beyond Romance* (New York: State University of New York Press, 2001), xi, 7, 55–56, 60–61.

23. William Shakespeare, "Sonnet 56," in *The Complete Works of William Shakespeare: The Alexander Text* (London: HarperCollins, 2006), 1371.

24. Allan Bloom, *Shakespeare on Love and Friendship* (Chicago: University of Chicago Press, 2000), 269–270.

25. Shakespeare, "Sonnet 147," in *The Complete Works*, 1385.

26. Here, of course, I refer to Shakespeare's Sonnet 18, which begins: "Shall I compare thee to a summer's day?" (in *The Complete Works*, 1365).

27. Irving Singer, *The Nature of Love*, vol. 1: *Plato to Luther*, 2nd ed. (Chicago: University of Chicago Press, 1984), 7. See also the section "What Is Love?" in part I.

28. Héloise, "Letter II," 31.

29. Singer, *The Nature of Love*, 1:7.

30. Stendhal, *On Love*, trans. Sophie Lewis (London: Hesperus Press, 2009), 6, 23, emphasis in original.

31. Ibid., 13–14.

32. Sigmund Freud, "'Civilized' Sexual Morality and Modern Nervous Illness," in *Sexuality and the Psychology of Love*, ed. Philip Rieff (1963; reprint, New York: Touchstone, 1997), 23.

33. Simone de Beauvoir, *The Second Sex*, trans. Constance Borde and Sheila Malovny-Chevallier (New York: Vintage Books, 2011), 706.

34. Ibid., 684, 693.

35. Ibid., 708, 691.

36. Maurice Merleau-Ponty, *The Primacy of Perception and Other Essays on Phenomenological Psychology, the Philosophy of Art, History, and Politics*, trans. William Cobb (Chicago: Northwestern University Press, 1964), 154.

37. Jean-Paul Sartre, *Being and Nothingness*, trans. Hazel E. Barnes (New York: Washington Square Press, 1992), 481–482, 479.

38. Maurice Merleau-Ponty, *Phenomenology of Perception*, trans. Colin Smith (New York: Routledge, 2002), 412.

39. Merleau-Ponty, *Primacy of Perception*, 154–155.

40. Ibid., 154.

41. Merleau-Ponty, *Phenomenology of Perception*, 413.

42. Ibid., 415.

43. The border between lovers is captured in another way by Luce Irigaray in her expression "I love *to* you," which prevents me from alienating my beloved's freedom. The preposition *to* designates a relation of indirection, of nonreduction; it is "the guarantor of two intentionalities: mine and yours" (*I Love to You: Sketch of a Possible Felicity in History*, trans. Alison Martin [New York: Routledge, 1996], 109–110).

44. Rose, *Love's Work*, 105.

45. Merleau-Ponty, *Primacy of Perception*, 154.

46. Virginia Woolf, *To the Lighthouse* (London: Grafton Books, 1977), 38.

47. Cixous, "Tancredi Continues," 79.

48. Morrison, *Beloved*, 272–273.

49. Hannah Arendt, *The Origins of Totalitarianism* (New York: Harcourt Brace, 1948), 301.

50. Arendt, *Love and Saint Augustine*, 18.

PART III. LIMITS

1. Hannah Arendt, *The Origins of Totalitarianism* (New York: Harcourt Brace, 1973), 301.
2. Lorna Crozier, *Small Beneath the Sky* (Vancouver: Greystone Books, 2009), 150, 121, 150.
3. Gillian Rose, *Love's Work: A Reckoning with Life* (New York: New York Review of Books, 1995), 61; subsequent page citations are given parenthetically in the text.
4. This question turns on its head an ethics of alterity as formulated by Emmanuel Levinas, whose emphasis on the other as one who "takes the bread from my mouth" fails to note the violent implications for the self whose bread is being taken. I am making a distinction between the gift and the sacrifice by noting that the giver of a gift is not necessarily emptied of self. I am arguing against Levinas: no one *should* take the bread from my mouth, for that would lead to masochism. See Emmanuel Levinas, *Totality and Infinity: An Essay on Exteriority*, trans. Alphonso Lingis (Pittsburg: Duquesne University Press, 1969).
5. Stephen Daldry, dir., *The Hours*, script by Michael Cunningham and David Hare, DVD (Hollywood: Paramount, 2003).
6. David Grossman, *Be My Knife*, trans. Vered Almog and Maya Gurantz (New York: Picador, 1998), 3; subsequent page citations are given parenthetically in the text.
7. Hélène Cixous and Mireille Calle-Gruber, *Rootprints: Memory and Life Writing*, trans. Eric Prenowitz (New York: Routledge, 1997), 108.
8. Virginia Woolf, *A Room of One's Own, Three Guineas*, ed. Michèle Barrett (London: Penguin Group, 2000), 32.
9. "Abuse," Dictionary.com, n.d., http://dictionary.reference.com/browse /abuse.
10. "Abuse," *Online Etymological Dictionary*, n.d., http://www.etymonline .com/index.php?term=abuse.
11. Julia Kristeva, *Tales of Love*, trans. Leon S. Roudiez (New York: Columbia University Press, 1987), 9.
12. I have addressed the moral status of victimhood and the political effects of victims who become perpetrators in *The Violence of Victimhood* (University Park: Penn State University Press, 2012).

13. Cixous and Calle-Gruber, *Rootprints*, 35.
14. I borrow this phrase from Hélène Cixous, *Twists and Turns in the Heart's Antarctic*, trans. Beverley Bie Brahic (Cambridge: Polity Press, 2014).
15. Barry Lopez, "Sliver of Sky," in *The Best American Essays 2014*, ed. John Jeremiah Sullivan (New York: Houghton Mifflin Harcourt, 2014), 137.
16. David Grossman, *Writing in the Dark: Essays on Literature and Politics*, trans. Jessica Cohen (New York: Farrar, Straus and Giroux, 2008), 44–45.
17. Ibid., 47, 48, 61.
18. Ibid., 48.
19. Cixous and Calle-Gruber, *Rootprints*, 30.
20. Grossman, *Writing in the Dark*, 54–55.
21. Miriam Toews, *All My Puny Sorrows* (Toronto: Knopf, 2014).
22. Ibid., 313–314.

PART IV. LOSS

1. This line refers to a poem by Rainer Maria Rilke, "Put Out My Eyes," in *Poems from the Book of Hours*, 2nd ed., trans. Babette Deutsch (New York: New Directions, 2009), 29.
2. I borrow the phrase "iron air" from Jane Hirshfield, "I Imagine Myself in Time," in *After: Poems* (New York: HarperCollins, 2006), 35.
3. Ibid.
4. Hannah Arendt, *The Life of the Mind* (New York: Harcourt, 1971), 185.
5. Julian Barnes, *Levels of Life* (Toronto: Vintage Canada, 2013), 67.
6. Ibid., 108.
7. Ibid., 70.
8. Ibid., 71.
9. Todd May, "Love and Death," in *Thinking About Love: Essays in Contemporary Continental Philosophy*, ed. Diane Enns and Antonio Calcagno (University Park: Penn State University Press, 2015), 28–30.
10. Slavoj Žižek, *Violence* (London: Picador, 2008), 50–51.
11. Hélène Cixous, "Love of the Wolf," trans. Keith Cohen, in *Stigmata: Escaping Texts* (1998; reprint, New York: Routledge, 2005), 72.

12. Patrick Lane, "A Red Bird Bearing on His Back an Empty Cup," in *Witness: Selected Poems 1962–2010* (Madeira Park, Canada: Harbour, 2010), 37.

13. "Even forgetting has its shape," writes Rainer Maria Rilke ("For Hans Carossa," in *The Poetry of Rilke*, trans. and ed. Edward Snow [New York: North Point Press, 2009], 573).

14. Ibid., 573.

15. In Jean Hatzfeld, *Life Laid Bare: The Survivors in Rwanda Speak* (New York: Other Press, 2007), 42–43.

16. David Grossman, *Falling Out of Time*, trans. Jessica Cohen (Toronto: McClelland & Stewart, 2014), 62, 139.

17. Ibid., 106.

18. Ibid., 140, italics in original.

19. David Grossman, *Arthur Miller Freedom to Write Lecture*, video, New York, 2007, http://www.c-span.org/video/?198061-1/freedom-write-lecture.

20. Grossman, *Falling Out of Time*, 192–193.

21. Friedrich Nietzsche, *Thus Spoke Zarathustra*, in *The Portable Nietzsche*, trans. and ed. Walter Kaufmann (New York: Penguin, 1976), 195.

22. Alain de Botton, *Essays in Love* (London: Picador Press, 2006), 198.

23. Martha C. Nussbaum, "Love and the Individual: Romantic Rightness and Platonic Aspiration," in *Love's Knowledge: Essays on Philosophy and Literature* (Oxford: Oxford University Press, 1990), 319–321.

24. Ibid., 318.

25. May, "Love and Death," 18.

26. Hannah Arendt, *The Origins of Totalitarianism* (New York: Harcourt Brace, 1973), 476.

27. Ibid., 475.

28. Vivian Gormick, "Letter from Greenwich Village," in *The Best American Essays 2014*, ed. John Jeremiah Sullivan (New York: Houghton Mifflin Harcourt, 2014), 65.

29. Gillian Rose, *Love's Work: A Reckoning with Life* (New York: New York Review of Books, 1995), 105–106.

30. Jacques Derrida and Jean Birnbaum, *Learning to Live Finally: The Last Interview*, trans. Pascale-Anne Brault and Michael Naas (2007; reprint, New York: Melville House, 2011), 46.

31. Ibid., 24.

32. Ibid., 24–25.

33. Ibid., 26.

34. Derrida acknowledges Walter Benjamin for emphasizing this distinction and notes its importance for his own work on the trace, the spectral, and mourning (ibid., 26).

35. Hélène Cixous, "My Algeriance, in other words: to depart not to arrive from Algeria," trans. Eric Prenowitz, in *Stigmata: Escaping Texts* (New York: Routledge, 1998), 170.

36. Derrida and Birnbaum, *Learning to Live Finally*, 29–30, my emphasis.

37. Ibid., 33.

38. Ibid., 32.

39. Ibid., 51, my emphasis.

40. Jacques Derrida, *Negotiations: Interventions and Interviews, 1971–2001*, ed. and trans. Elizabeth Rottenberg (Stanford: Stanford University Press, 2002), 11, 13.

41. Rose, *Love's Work*, 79, 77, 74.

42. Jacques Derrida and Geoffrey Bennington, "Circumfession," quoted in Jean Birnbaum, introduction to Derrida and Birnbaum, *Learning to Live Finally*, 17.

43. Rose, *Love's Work*, 100, 94–96.

44. Ibid., 144.

AFTERWORD

1. Aristotle, *Nicomachean Ethics*, trans. Terence Irwin, 2nd ed. (Indianapolis, Ind.: Hackett, 1999), book VIII: I, 1155a.

2. Ibid.

3. Ibid., 1156a–1157b.

4. Simone de Beauvoir, *The Second Sex*, trans. Constance Borde and Sheila Malovny-Chevallier (New York: Vintage Books, 2011), 693.

BIBLIOGRAPHY

Arendt, Hannah. *The Life of the Mind*. New York: Harcourt, 1971.

——. *Love and Saint Augustine*. Edited by Joanna Vecchiarelli Scott and Judith Chelius Stark. Chicago: University of Chicago Press, 1996.

——. *The Origins of Totalitarianism*. New York: Harcourt Brace, 1973.

Aristotle. *Nicomachean Ethics*. Translated by Terence Irwin. 2nd ed. Indianapolis, Ind.: Hackett, 1999.

Atwood, Margaret. *Alias Grace*. Toronto: McClelland & Stewart, 1996.

Augustine. *Confessions*. Translated by Henry Chadwick. Oxford: Oxford University Press, 1991.

Barnes, Julian. *Levels of Life*. Toronto: Vintage Canada, 2013.

Birnbaum, Jean. Introduction to Jacques Derrida and Jean Birnbaum, *Learning to Live Finally: The Last Interview*, translated by Pascale-Anne Brault and Michael Naas, 9–17. 2007. Reprint. New York: Melville House, 2011.

Bloom, Allan. *Shakespeare on Love and Friendship*. Chicago: University of Chicago Press, 2000.

Carson, Anne. *Eros the Bittersweet*. London: Dalkey Archive Press, 1998.

Chadwick, Henry. Introduction to Augustine, *Confessions*, translated by Henry Chadwick, ix–xxvi. Oxford: Oxford University Press, 1991.

Cixous, Hélène. *"Coming to Writing" and Other Essays*. Edited by Deborah Jenson. Translated by Sarah Cornell, Deborah Jenson, Ann Liddle, and Susan Sellers. Cambridge, Mass.: Harvard University Press, 1991.

——. "Love of the Wolf." Translated by Keith Cohen. In *Stigmata: Escaping Texts*, 70–82. 1998. Reprint. New York: Routledge, 2005.

——. "My Algeriance, in other words: to depart not to arrive from Algeria." Translated by Eric Prenowitz. In *Stigmata: Escaping Texts*, 153–172. New York: Routledge, 1998.

——. "Tancredi Continues." In *"Coming to Writing" and Other Essays*, edited by Deborah Jenson, translated by Sarah Cornell, Deborah Jenson, Ann Liddle, and Susan Sellers, 78–103. Cambridge, Mass.: Harvard University Press, 1991.

——. *Twists and Turns in the Heart's Antarctic*. Translated by Beverley Bie Brahic. Cambridge: Polity Press, 2014.

Cixous, Hélène, and Mireille Calle-Gruber. *Rootprints: Memory and Life Writing*. Translated by Eric Prenowitz. New York: Routledge, 1997.

Crozier, Lorna. *Small Beneath the Sky*. Vancouver: Greystone Books, 2009.

Daldry, Stephen, dir. *The Hours*. Screenplay by Michael Cunningham and David Hare. DVD. Hollywood: Paramount, 2003.

De Beauvoir, Simone. *The Second Sex*. Translated by Constance Borde and Sheila Malovny-Chevallier. New York: Vintage Books, 2011.

De Botton, Alain. *Essays in Love*. London: Picador, 2006.

Derrida, Jacques. *Negotiations: Interventions and Interviews, 1971–2001*. Edited and translated by Elizabeth Rottenberg. Stanford: Stanford University Press, 2002.

——. *Of Hospitality*. Translated by Rachel Bowlby. Stanford: Stanford University Press, 2000.

Derrida, Jacques, and Jean Birnbaum. *Learning to Live Finally: The Last Interview*. Translated by Pascale-Anne Brault and Michael Naas. 2007. Reprint. New York: Melville House, 2011.

Dillon, M. C. *Beyond Romance*. New York: State University of New York Press, 2001.

Enns, Diane. *The Violence of Victimhood*. University Park: Penn State University Press, 2012.

Foucault, Michel. *The History of Sexuality: An Introduction*. Translated by Robert Hurley. New York: Random House, 1978.

Freud, Sigmund. "'Civilized' Sexual Morality and Modern Nervous Illness." In *Sexuality and the Psychology of Love*, edited by Philip Rieff, 10–30. 1963. Reprint. New York: Touchstone, 1997.

Gormick, Vivian. "Letter from Greenwich Village." In *The Best American Essays 2014*, edited by John Jeremiah Sullivan, 49–65. New York: Houghton Mifflin Harcourt, 2014.

Grossman, David. *Arthur Miller Freedom to Write Lecture*. New York, 2007. http://www.cspan.org/video/?198061-1/freedom-write-lecture.

——. *Be My Knife*. Translated by Vered Almog and Maya Gurantz. New York: Picador, 1998.

——. *Falling Out of Time*. Translated by Jessica Cohen. Toronto: McClelland & Stewart. 2014.

——. *Writing in the Dark: Essays on Literature and Politics*. Translated by Jessica Cohen. New York: Farrar, Straus and Giroux, 2008.

Hatzfeld, Jean. *Life Laid Bare: The Survivors in Rwanda Speak*. New York: Other Press, 2007.

Herzen, Alexander. *My Past and Thoughts: The Memoirs of Alexander Herzen*. Translated by Constance Garnett. Abridged ed. New York: Knopf, 1973.

Hirshfield, Jane. "I Imagine Myself in Time." In *After: Poems*, 35. New York: HarperCollins, 2006.

Irigaray, Luce. *I Love to You: Sketch of a Possible Felicity in History*. Translated by Alison Martin. New York: Routledge, 1996.

——. "Sorcerer Love, a Reading of Plato's *Symposium*, Diotima's Speech." Translated by Eleanor H. Kuykendall. *Hypatia* 3, no. 3 (1989): 32–44.

——. *This Sex Which Is Not One*. Translated by Catherine Porter with Carolyn Burke. Ithaca: Cornell University Press, 1977.

Kant, Immanuel. *The Metaphysics of Morals*. Translated and edited by Mary J. Gregor. Cambridge: Cambridge University Press, 1996.

Kristeva, Julia. *Tales of Love*. Translated by Leon S. Roudiez. New York: Columbia University Press, 1987.

Lane, Patrick. "A Red Bird Bearing on His Back an Empty Cup." In *Witness: Selected Poems 1962–2010*, 36–37. Madeira Park, Canada: Harbour, 2010.

Levinas, Emmanuel. *Totality and Infinity: An Essay on Exteriority*. Translated by Alphonso Lingis. Pittsburg: Duquesne University Press, 1969.

Lilburn, Tim. *Living in the World as If It Were Home: Essays*. Dunvegan, Canada: Cormorant Books, 1999.

Lopez, Barry. "Sliver of Sky." In *The Best American Essays 2014*, edited by John Jeremiah Sullivan, 122–139. New York: Houghton Mifflin Harcourt, 2014.

The Love Letters of Abelard and Héloise. London: Dent, 1901. http://sacred-texts.com/chr/aah/index.htm.

Marion, Jean-Luc. *The Erotic Phenomenon*. Translated by Stephen E. Lewis. Chicago: University of Chicago Press, 2007.

May, Todd. "Love and Death." In *Thinking About Love: Essays in Contemporary Continental Philosophy*, edited by Diane Enns and Antonio Calcagno, 17–30. University Park: Penn State University Press, 2015.

Merleau-Ponty, Maurice. *Phenomenology of Perception*. Translated by Colin Smith. New York: Routledge, 2002.

——. *The Primacy of Perception and Other Essays on Phenomenological Psychology, the Philosophy of Art, History, and Politics*. Translated by William Cobb. Chicago: Northwestern University Press, 1964.

Morrison, Toni. *Beloved*. New York: Penguin Books, 1987.

The New Oxford Annotated Bible. Revised Standard Version. Edited by Herbert G. May and Bruce M. Metzger. New York: Oxford University Press, 1962.

Nietzsche, Friedrich. *Thus Spoke Zarathustra*. In *The Portable Nietzsche*, translated and edited by Walter Kaufmann, 115–439. New York: Penguin, 1976.

Nussbaum, Martha C. "Love and the Individual: Romantic Rightness and Platonic Aspiration." In *Love's Knowledge: Essays on Philosophy and Literature*, 314–334. Oxford: Oxford University Press, 1990.

——. "Steerforth's Arm: Love and the Moral Point of View." In *Love's Knowledge: Essays on Philosophy and Literature*, 335–364. Oxford: Oxford University Press, 1990.

O'Connor, Flannery. "A Temple of the Holy Ghost." In *A Good Man Is Hard to Find, and Other Stories*, 85–101. New York: Harcourt, 1955.

Plato. *Symposium*. Translated by Alexander Nehemas and Paul Woodruff. Indianapolis, Ind.: Hackett, 1989.

Rilke, Rainer Maria. "For Hans Carossa." In *The Poetry of Rilke*, translated and edited by Edward Snow, 573. New York: North Point Press, 2009.

——. "Put Out My Eyes." In *Poems from the Book of Hours*, 2nd ed., translated by Babette Deutsch, 29. New York: New Directions, 2009.

Rose, Gillian. *Love's Work: A Reckoning with Life*. New York: New York Review of Books, 1995.

Sappho. *If Not, Winter: Fragments of Sappho*. Translated by Anne Carson. New York: Vintage, 2003.

Sartre, Jean-Paul. *Being and Nothingness.* Translated by Hazel E. Barnes. New York: Washington Square Press, 1992.

Shakespeare, William. *The Complete Works of William Shakespeare: The Alexander Text.* London: HarperCollins, 2006.

Singer, Irving. *The Nature of Love.* Vol. 1: *Plato to Luther.* 2nd ed. Chicago: University of Chicago Press, 1984.

Sontag, Susan. *As Consciousness Is Harnessed to Flesh: Journals and Notebooks, 1964–1980.* Edited by David Rieff. New York: Farrar, Straus and Giroux, 2012.

Stendhal. *On Love.* Translated by Sophie Lewis. London. Hesperus Press, 2009.

Teresa of Ávila. *The Life of Teresa of Jesus: The Autobiography of Teresa of Ávila.* Translated and edited by E. Allison Peers. New York: Doubleday, 1991.

Toews, Miriam. *All My Puny Sorrows.* Toronto: Knopf, 2014.

Tóibín, Colm. "Roaming the Greenwood." *London Review of Books* 29, no. 2 (1999): 12–16. http://www.lrb.co.uk/v21/n02/colm-toibin/roaming-the -greenwood.

———. *The Testament of Mary.* Toronto: McClelland & Stewart, 2012.

Woolf, Virginia. *A Room of One's Own, Three Guineas.* Edited by Michèle Barrett. London: Penguin Group, 2000.

———. *To the Lighthouse.* London: Grafton Books, 1977.

World Health Organization. *Female Genital Mutilation Fact Sheet.* Updated February 2014. http://www.who.int/mediacentre/factsheets/fs241/en/.

Žižek, Slavoj. *Violence.* London: Picador, 2008.

INDEX

humility, 129
husbands, 12–14

ideal couple love, 6–7
idealization: beautification and, 62;
    death and, 136; of love, 37
idolatrous love, 68
immortality, 134, 154, 155
imperfect love, 75
incest, 98
incitement, 166n6
individuality, 145
infants: autonomy and, 72; crazy
    love and, 51; loss and, 123–24
infatuation, 62
inheritance, 153
intense emotions, xii
intercourse, 23. *See also* sex
intimacy, 92
intimate love, 55
invulnerability, 73
Irigaray, Luce, 28, 168n41, 170n43
irrationality, 38
isolation: emotional, 147;
    psychological, 147

Jesus, 15, 27
Joseph (biblical figure), 16

Kafka, Franz, xiv, xv
Kant, Immanuel, 27; pathological
    love and, 35; will and, 37
kindness, 163
knife metaphor, 88–89, 90
Kristeva, Julia, 27, 98

language: conventions of, xii; of
    happy love, 45, 83; of liberal
    autonomy, 75; love for, 153;
    movement and, 46; shared, 68
Leah (biblical figure), 16
leaving, 119–20
Levinas, Emmanuel, 171n4
liberal autonomy, 8; language of, 75
liberal ideals, of romantic love, 81
liberal love, 6–7
lifedeath, 151
life-preservation instinct, 153
Lilburn, Tim, xvi
lived time, 132
living alone, 147
living death, 151, 156
living on (*fortleben*), 151, 152, 153, 154
living through (*überleben*), 151, 154
localized loss, 130
loneliness, 149, 164; aging and, 147;
    desire and, 148; human condition
    and, 146, 147
longevity, 6
Lopez, Barry, 111
loss: infants and, 123–24; localized,
    130; of virginity, 23–24; writing
    and, 3. *See also* grief; mourning
Lot (biblical figure), 166n10
lovability, xvi
love, 4–9; as blind, 62, 64; brief,
    60; carnal, 53; codependent, 68;
    conjugal, 14; crazy, 51; diseased,
    6; first, 123; formulas for, xi;
    friendship, 5; ideal couple, 6–7;
    idealization of, 37; idolatrous, 68;

objectification, of women, 44
O'Connor, Flannery, 11
Old Testament, 12
openness, 70
Othello (Shakespeare), 113

pain, 72, 80; masochism and, 107,
126; of self-sacrifice, 66
paranoia, 113
passion, 54
past-present, 131
pathological love, 65–68;
attachments and, 67; de Beauvoir
and, 66; Kant and, 35
pathology, love as, 8
patriarchy, 68
Paul, 9–11, 12–13, 14, 17, 26, 28, 37
perfection, 81
Philintus, 32–33
"Philosophy of Love and Sex, The"
(course), 43
philosophy proper, xii
physical abuse, 100, 102
Plato, xii, 37, 50, 55, 63, 65; arrogance
of, 26; body and, 30, 46; Diotima
and, 29; discipleship and, 27;
erotic love and, 45; vulgar love
and, 47
pleasure: clitoris and, 23–24; guilt
and, 9; love stories and, xi;
masochism and, 107
poetry, xi, xii, xiv, 46–47
practical love, 35
presence, unconditional, 51
prohibition, 166n6

promiscuity, 44
propaganda, 104
prosthesis, xiv
prostitution, 98
psychological abuse, 110
psychological isolation, 147
psychotherapy, 8

Rachel (biblical figure), 16
rage, 4, 87
rape, 97, 98
reason, emotion and, 33
rebounding, 143
reciprocity, 83, 84
rejection, 116, 126
relationships, types of, 5
relativism, 44–45
religious cults, 104
repose, 150
resentment, 4
resilience, 137
respect: fear and, 14; friendship and,
163
Rilke, Rainer Maria, 137
risk: paradox of, 105–8; of
vulnerability, 106
romance, 61; beauty and, 62;
industry, 68
romantic love, xv, 5, 51, 55, 60; as
adolescent, 58; crystallization
and, 63–64; liberal ideals of, 81;
liberal love and, 6–7; mortality
and, 134; myths of, 43, 44; as
threat, 35
rooting, 51